RECLAIMING
FRANCIS

"Msgr. Murphy offers readers an insightful look into the significance and legacy of St. Francis of Assisi for the Church and world today according to the New Evangelization and the wonderfully hopeful election of Pope Francis. This book, the first of its kind, is sure to inspire rich conversation and deep reflection on the meaning of Christian discipleship in our time and challenge us to 'preach by our deeds' just as [both] the saint and the pope named Francis did."

Daniel P. Horan, O.F.M.
Author of *Dating God*

"The Church must continue to re-propose its message for every new generation. To do this, word and witness have to be one and the same. In this book, Msgr. Charles Murphy offers us two superb examples of this authentic witness in St. Francis of Assisi and Pope Francis, thereby making a significant contribution to contemporary discussions of the new evangelization."

Maureen E. Sullivan, O.P.
Author of *The Road to Vatican II*

"Charles M. Murphy presents a series of thoughtful reflections on key aspects in the life and spirituality of St. Francis of Assisi. He proposes the great thirteenth-century mendicant friar as a model of gospel living for our time. This work provides an important insight into the kind of authentic witness required to carry out the New Evangelization mandated by the recent international synod of bishops and into the appeal of the newly elected pope, the first to take the name of Francis."

Catherine E. Clifford
Coauthor of *Keys to the Council*

Reclaiming Francis

How the Saint
and the Pope
Are Renewing
the Church

Charles M. Murphy

ave maria press AMP notre dame, indiana

Founded in 1865, Ave Maria Press is a ministry of the United States Province of Holy Cross.

www.avemariapress.com

Paperback ISBN-13 978-1-59471-478-8

E-book ISBN-13 978-1-59471-479-5

Cover image © Thinkstock.com.

Cover and text design by Brian C. Conley.

Printed and bound in the United States of America.

Library of Congress Cataloging-in-Publication Data is available.

For Pope Francis, Jorge Mario Bergoglio,
who has taken the name of St. Francis of Assisi
to preach the Gospel in our day,
with admiration and support.

CONTENTS

FOREWORD

For me, participating in the conclave that elected Pope Francis was a Pentecost experience right out of the Acts of the Apostles. Catholics all over the world prayed for the Church, the cardinals, and the conclave so that the Holy Spirit would guide us. I have no doubt that all our prayers were answered. In the gospels, Jesus is always seeking those at the periphery and bringing them to center stage. By having a pope from the Southern Hemisphere the Church is doing that. I am sure that Pope Francis will be a great stimulus and an encouragement to our brothers and sisters in those parts of the world.

I am also convinced that Pope Francis's unswerving devotion to the poor and the social gospel of the Church will touch the hearts of many in the secularized countries of Europe and North America, helping them to see the Church in a new light. Our love for the poor is never just philanthropy; it is rather the evangelical poverty that inspired St. Francis to kiss the leper, to give all his wealth to the poor, to see Lady Poverty as freedom from the shackles of wealth. In the context of faith, embracing the spirit of poverty is an expression of humility, seeking the last place at the table in order to be near to Christ who has come to wash our feet. We are called to the detachment that allows us to recognize the poor and the suffering as an icon of the crucified Lord—as a manifestation of his presence in the world.

I am confident that Pope Francis's love for the poor and his passion for the social gospel will help galvanize the Church to greater fidelity to the gospel and a renewed commitment to building a civilization of love. We do these works of mercy, caring for the poor and needy, because we are Catholics and it is what we are supposed to do. I often reflect on the occasion in the Gospel when Jesus took his disciples to the Temple to point out to them the poor widow who dropped her last penny in the collection basket. Jesus didn't say anything to the woman; he didn't give her the money back. He simply wanted his disciples to see and appreciate the faith and generosity of the poor widow.

Monsignor Murphy spent ten years in Italy as a seminarian and later as rector of the Pontifical North American College. During those years he grew in his love for St. Francis of Assisi and became convinced that St. Francis can guide us in the needed rebuilding of the Church in our day and the repair of our secular society. He had completed his book setting forth St. Francis's program of renewal and reform when our new Holy Father took the name of Francis out of the same conviction. Monsignor Murphy was thus able to incorporate into this book the vision of Pope Francis, which exemplifies so well the witness of St. Francis. May this book contribute to the new evangelization deeply needed at this particular moment of history.

Cardinal Seán P. O'Malley, O.F.M. Cap.
Archbishop of Boston

Preface

A few weeks before Pope Francis's election as the new pope, I had completed this manuscript on St. Francis of Assisi and the new evangelization—or so I thought. Then came this amazing coincidence: the new pope embraced Francis as the model for his pontificate. I prefer to think that this was not really a coincidence but rather a shared vision of how the Church can be renewed and how people today can be helped to find faith once again.

I want to express my gratitude for the gracious Foreword to this book contributed by Cardinal Seán O'Malley O.F.M., Cap., archbishop of Boston. As a close collaborator of Pope Francis, Cardinal O'Malley shares his vision for the rebuilding of the Church and its Franciscan inspiration. A mutual friend, Cardinal William Baum, once said to me, "Seán O'Malley is the finest priest I know." I have reason to see why.

During the past twenty years I have been working with permanent deacons as their diocesan director. St. Francis himself was a deacon who sought to be "a living gospel for all to hear." May all deacons of today's Church who have taken Francis as their model carry out their mission to "believe what you read, preach what you believe, and practice what you preach."

Introduction

A summer ago I spent time exploring New Mexico for the first time. I had two reasons for going. I wanted to attend the Santa Fe Opera, founded by the late John Crosby, a cousin of parishioners of mine. I also had been looking forward to visiting close friends who have a home in Santa Fe. She is an artist, he an aspiring writer after a long career in business.

Together we attended two operas in the spectacular setting of the new opera house with its open sides and stage that reveal the sun as it sets. Besides spending time in Santa Fe, we visited Taos to see Ghost Ranch, the home of Georgia O'Keeffe, and stayed at the former home of Mabel Dodge Luhan, who came to Taos in 1918 from New York. There she entertained D. H. Lawrence and his wife, Freida; Ansel Adams; Martha Graham; Georgia O'Keeffe herself; and many others in those comfortable rooms.

My friends were anxious for me to spend some time with their son and daughter-in-law who live in Santa Fe year-round. For years the son has devoted himself to environmental causes, making regular lobbying trips to Washington and heading up a nonprofit organization promoting the ecological well-being of the Southwest. He has taken a longtime interest in the Rio Grande River, which he has been trying to preserve as a single, magnificent ecosystem. The son's wife teaches part-time. One of the courses she teaches is on nonviolent techniques, with a particular emphasis on nonviolent speech. Both were baptized Catholics. She once taught in a Catholic elementary school, but neither has much contact with Catholicism today.

The five of us met several times during my stay. Our best conversation was on a Sunday morning at the young couple's home on the outskirts of Santa Fe, a spacious single-floor dwelling with an ample veranda opening out onto the vegetable gardens from which they harvest much of their food. The brunch was on the veranda, and the main course was a vegetable quiche. Both are vegetarians.

My two friends and I attended Mass at the Cathedral of San Francisco de Asis in the city and then proceeded to drive out to our brunch invitation. In my tour of the house I visited the separate zones they have created for their private time: a place to do crafts and meditate for her, and likewise a meditation room for him where he could also practice his cello.

I was impressed with their spiritual view of life, their attachment to the landscape, and their commitment to social justice. Over the course of our leisurely conversation, I asked if they knew much about St. Francis of Assisi, with whom they seemed to share so much. They said they did not.

Perhaps the new way of evangelizing is not so much through confrontation and argument but through conversation, dialogue, and affirmation, a way that allows us to reach out to people similar to my friends in New Mexico who already have a spiritual life and who can be introduced to Christ by someone such as St. Francis. St Francis seems the perfect guide to lead so many in our times into deeper waters.

Originally a phrase used by Jesus (Lk 5:4), "Deeper waters," is an image Blessed John Paul II evoked in his apostolic letter on the two thousandth anniversary of the birth of Christ. He continued: "Despite widespread secularization, there is a widespread demand for spirituality."[1] We are called to engage that demand for spiritual truths in spite of the overarching movement toward secularization. St. Francis pioneered this method in a different context during his conversations with the sultan of Egypt in the extreme situation of the Third Crusade against Islam. Whereas most would have been overwhelmed by the surface differences, Francis cast into deeper waters.

In proclaiming a "Year of Faith" from October 2012 to November 2013, Pope Emeritus Benedict XVI called a synod on what is being called the "new evangelization." New evangelization is defined as a renewed dynamism, inspired by the Holy Spirit, which allows the Church to repropose its message, especially to those who, like my friends, have drifted away. As indicated in a synodal document, "The new evangelization is primarily directed to these people, so that they can rediscover the beauty of their Christian faith and the joy of a personal relationship with the Lord Jesus in the church and in the community of the faithful."[2]

Among the synod's final propositions is the following:

> The universal call to holiness is constitutive of the new evangelization that sees the saints as effective models of the variety and forms in which this vocation can be realized. What is common in the varied stories of holiness is the following of Christ expressed in a life of

faith active in charity which is a privileged proclamation of the gospel.[3]

In this book I propose St. Francis of Assisi (1186–1226) as a preeminent saintly model for the new evangelization. He inspired in his own lifetime what is generally recognized as the greatest spiritual renewal the Church has ever experienced in her long history. Pope Paul VI, who originally pointed to evangelization as the Church's essential mission, said that "people today listen more to witnesses than to teachers. Witnesses to Jesus Christ demonstrate their faith especially by the witness of poverty and detachment, of freedom in the face of the powers of this world, that is, by the witness of a holy life."[4] St. Francis of Assisi, known in his own day as *il poverello*, "the little poor one," is just such a needed witness and model. Francis achieved this astounding and still-normative spiritual renewal precisely because his personal holiness was founded upon poverty of spirit and resistance to the prevailing culture of his time, a culture that in so many ways resembles our own. According to his official biographer, St. Bonaventure, Francis "is the outstanding follower of Jesus crucified."[5]

The ultimate reason for Francis's appeal is that he resembles Christ. Francis fascinates because Christ is fascinating. Today many are careful to eat well, rest, diet, exercise, and expand their minds in cultural pursuits—all of which can be appropriate—but often these same people neglect their spiritual needs. When they notice the spiritual emptiness inside of them, many look for spiritual fulfillment anywhere but in Christ. They feel they "know" Christ, they understand Christianity, and, dissatisfied, they want something more. But often they do not know Christ, for they have encountered at most a child's version of him.

This was the case with my friends in New Mexico, and that is why I wanted to introduce the actual Christ to them by means of St. Francis of Assisi.

In the first part of this book I explore the similarities of St. Francis's world and ours in terms of the challenge of evangelization. In the second part I lay out a program to accomplish this evangelization rooted in ways St. Francis exemplified. As will be clear, that program requires not mere pious words or new Church organizations; it is the very countercultural challenge of living out and bearing witness to Jesus' invitation: "Come, follow me" (Mt 19:21).

The New Testament definition of a disciple is "one who follows." The disciples literally lived with their master, learning his ways by observing the smallest details of his life—following him around. Since Christ's resurrection, the New Testament meaning of being a disciple comes to be not "to follow" as much as "to imitate." St. Paul, for example, never speaks of *following* Christ but of *imitating* him, taking on his mind.

> Have among yourselves the same [mind] attitude that is also yours in Christ Jesus who, though he was in the form of God, did not regard equality with God something to be grasped. Rather, he emptied himself, taking the form of a slave, coming in human likeness; and found human in appearance, he humbled himself, becoming obedient to death, even death on a cross. (Phil 2:5–8)

As I make clear in the second part of this book, this mind of Christ includes the priority of God, the preferential love of the poor, voluntary poverty, care for creation, and the pursuit of peace. These are the ways by which the Church will be rebuilt.

PART ONE

ST. FRANCIS'S
WORLD AND OURS

ONE

A Saint for Today

St. Francis admirably fulfills the three criteria proposed by the synod's working document on the new evangelization, for (a) he makes the Christian life seem plausible and attractive even in the circumstances of today, (b) the witness of his life manifests the possibility that the world itself can be changed, and (c) he shows that this all can be done in complete union with the Church.

In the 1920s the eminent British journalist, fiction writer, and convert to Catholicism Gilbert Keith Chesterton wrote a book on St. Francis of Assisi, a book that has been in print ever since. In many ways it is a typically Chesterton production: ruminative and digressive. I picture Chesterton dictating the book to his stenographer with various reference works scattered around him on the floor. The book betrays the prejudices of the time, particularly with regard to Muslims, but basically Chesterton gets Francis right.

In the end his audience is the same as mine. He says he is not writing for the liberal skeptics who admire an image of Francis of Assisi who is a humanitarian hero and lover of birds and animals, "a saint without God." Neither is his intended audience those religious devotees who are comfortable with stigmata and fights against dragons. Chesterton writes "for the modern outsider and enquirer," as he himself once was, who may regard aspects of Francis's life as attractive but also somewhat remote and even repulsive—in other words, "the ordinary modern person, sympathetic but skeptical."[1] This skepticism abounds. During a recent visit to Assisi, our guide, a modern Italian woman, pointed out with a slight smile the thorn bush onto which St. Francis supposedly hurled himself to avert an episode of sexual desire.

Chesterton confronts the doubting modern mind directly. He shows us Francis, the all too human, self-described lover and troubadour, but enunciates the fact that his first love was God. The point to his life story, then, the precipice to which everything else leads, is Francis's embrace of the cross. For Chesterton, Francis is nothing less than the Mirror of Christ whose counsels of perfection, followed to the letter by *il poverello* and his companions, were intended "to astonish and awaken the world."[2]

Contemporary author Joseph Bottum sets forth much the same insight—this time about the Church reflecting divinity—in a column he wrote soon after Pope Francis's election. He writes:

> The Catholic Church is not one of the last surviving medieval institutions in the world. Even in the Middle Ages, it was old, for the church is the world's only surviving ancient institution—born in a world shaped by Alexander's conquests, deriving from a time of Roman rule. And we will never understand it, never grasp its fundamentally counter-cultural nature, unless we recognize this fact. In every age, somewhere in the church, there flashes into the present moment a religious claim—a divine revelation, say its believers—from the ancient world.[3]

Blessed John Paul II, who selected Assisi as the pilgrimage site for his first assembly of world religious leaders praying for peace in 1986, said of Francis that he was "great in the thirteenth century but he has become even more important today." Already considered a saint at the time of his death, October 3, 1226, Francis was canonized only two years later in 1228 by Pope Gregory IX, who said of him on that occasion, "He shone in his days as a morning star in the midst of clouds."[4]

St. Elizabeth, the young widow of the king of Hungary, became a secular Franciscan and was renowned for her love of the poor before her early death in 1231—only five years after the death of St. Francis himself. This exemplifies how quickly widespread was the spiritual renewal he inspired.

Like us, Francis lived in a time when the Church was in a new situation and ripe for renewal. The twelfth century saw the revival of arts and learning across Europe, including the vernacular poetry associated with the troubadours. The election at the age of thirty-seven of the noble and learned Innocent III saw the initial establishment of the papal states and an immense enlargement of the papal prestige; Innocent was the first to call himself "vicar of Christ." Although his sponsorship of the Fourth Crusade to liberate the Holy Land from the Muslims proved to be a debacle, Innocent's convocation of the Fourth Lateran Council in 1206 was, according to the historian John O'Malley, "one of the largest and most impressive assemblies in the Middle Ages and the largest council in the history of the church up to that point."[5] Like the Second Vatican Council, the Fourth Lateran Council of 1215 was a council concerned with reformation. It created what ever after has been called the "Easter duty": to remain in good standing, all Catholics must receive Holy Communion and, if necessary, go to confession at least once per year.

Beyond the "Easter duty," Innocent's greatest lasting influence upon the Church was his encouragement of the creation of new religious orders by St. Dominic and St. Francis. A new body of ministers thus sprang into being alongside the regular clergy and outside of the conventional parish-based structure. Dominicans and Franciscans were fundamentally orders of preachers who spoke the Gospel to the people in their own language. Their influence has been felt ever since. They grew quickly in this era of renewal, and an amazing seventeen thousand friars of Francis's new order gathered from all over Europe for the first chapter order in 1260.

In the popular imagination, St. Francis's lasting legacy lies in his relationship to "nature" or the environment. The American ecologist Lynn White has written, "The greatest spiritual revolutionary in Western history, St. Francis proposed an alternative view of nature and man's relation to it."[6] The Church confirmed this crucial characteristic in 1980 when Blessed John Paul II made him patron saint of ecology. The religious historian Marina Warner, speaking for many, wrote, "The Franciscan spirit continues to be considered by agnostics and atheists, as well as believers, as the most genuine expression of Christ's teaching ever approved by the Vatican."[7]

POPE FRANCIS

At the age of seventy-six, on March 13, 2013, Cardinal Jorge Mario Bergoglio of Buenos Aires was elected pope. He is the first to come, as he said, "from the edge of the world," as well as the first Jesuit and the first to take the name Francis.

A pope selects his name to announce a vision for his pontificate. Popes John Paul I and II saw themselves as carrying forward the program of renewal and reform initiated by Pope John XXIII, who summoned the Second Vatican Council, which was completed by Pope Paul VI. Pope Benedict XVI, on the other hand, surveying the increasing secularization of Europe symbolized by the omission of any reference to God in the European Union's proposed constitution, selected the name of the great founder of monasticism in the West, Benedict of Nursia, a saint who shaped Western civilization for more than a millennium. And, in typical fashion, this is how Pope Francis explained the selection of his name to the six thousand journalists who had covered the conclave that elected him:

> Some people wanted to know why the Bishop of Rome wished to be called Francis. Some thought of Francis Xavier, Francis De Sales, and also Francis of Assisi. I will tell you the story. During the election, I was seated next to the Archbishop Emeritus of São Paolo and Prefect Emeritus of the Congregation for the Clergy, Cardinal Claudio Hummes: a good friend, a good friend! When things were looking dangerous, he encouraged me. And when the votes reached two thirds, there was the usual applause, because the Pope had been elected. And he gave me a hug and a kiss, and said: "Don't forget the poor!" And those words came to me: the poor, the poor. Then, right away, thinking of the poor, I thought of Francis of Assisi. Then I thought of all the wars, as the votes were still being counted, till the end. Francis is also the man of peace.

That is how the name came into my heart: Francis of Assisi. For me, he is the man of poverty, the man of peace, the man who loves and protects creation; these days we do not have a very good relationship with creation, do we? He is the man who gives us this spirit of peace, the poor man. . . . How I would like a Church which is poor and for the poor![8]

At his first Sunday recitation of the Angelus in St. Peter's Square, Pope Francis added another reason, saying he chose the name of the patron saint of Italy to reinforce "my spiritual link with this land where, as you know, my family has its origins." His Italian roots, also emphasized by the selection of this name, reinforce his conception of the papacy as being, fundamentally, the bishop of Rome who presides in charity over the universal Church.

"How I would like a church which is poor and for the poor!" What more concise description of a pontificate could we have? The new evangelization, a pastoral priority of the Church in our time, can now be guided—front and center—by the example of St. Francis of Assisi.

There is no question Jorge Bergoglio is a humble man. His episcopal motto, selected not from the Bible but from the English Church Father Bede, is a good example. It reads, "*Miserando atque eligendo*" (having pity on him, he chose him). St. Bede, who lived in the eighth century, coined this phrase in his exegesis of the call of Matthew to become an apostle (Mt 9:9–13). Bede explains that Jesus saw Matthew not just in his appearance and profession but with merciful understanding. This conversion of one sinner gave other sinners an example of repentance and pardon. Bede concludes, "No sooner was he converted than

Matthew drew after him a whole crowd of sinners along the road to salvation."

Pope Francis's first appearance after his election on the balcony of St. Peter's was full of surprises. At first he simply stood there, looking at the applauding crowd. He didn't wave; he just looked. After a few suspenseful minutes, he called the crowd to silence and asked them to pray for him silently as he bowed his head. They did so, with all the media watching in amazement. He wore no stole or ermine-fringed cape, but only the white cassock which has been used by the popes since St. Pius V, who continued to wear his white Dominican habit. His shoes were black, as were his trousers. On his wrist was a black plastic watch, and he wore no cuff links. This simplified garb was not merely a momentary symbol; his commitment to simplicity has not changed since his election as pope. His first words were, "*Buena sera*" (Good evening). His last were, "Good night and sleep well," recalling Blessed John XXIII's colloquial conclusion to a similar crowd in the square: "Kiss your babies for me."

The next day in the Sistine Chapel, during the Mass he concelebrated with the cardinals who elected him, Pope Francis set aside the prepared Latin homily. Speaking spontaneously and standing behind the lectern, he summarized the lectionary's readings for the day with three verbs: walking, building, and professing. "The thing, however, is not so easy, because in walking, in building and in professing there are sometimes shake-ups," he said. He continued,

> The same Peter who confessed Jesus Christ says, "You are the Christ, the Son of the living God. I will follow you, but let us not speak of the cross." This has nothing

to do with it," he says. "I will follow you in other ways that do not include the cross." When we walk without the cross, when we build without the cross, and when we profess Christ without the cross, we are not disciples of the Lord. We are worldly, we are bishops, priests, cardinals, popes, but not disciples of the Lord.

I would like that all of us, after these days of grace, might have the courage—the courage—to walk in the presence of the Lord with the cross of the Lord, to build the church on the blood of the Lord which was shed upon the cross, and to profess the one glory, Christ crucified. In this way the church will go forward.[9]

True to his namesake Francis, the pope began his pontificate by preaching the cross as the means by which we will rebuild the Church and repair the city. Like all of his homilies, this one was brief and from the heart, based on scripture and containing a strong evangelical call to conversion. Of course, this cannot just be a matter of words; it must be carried out by example. Is it then surprising that, at least in the time following his election, Pope Francis chose the *Domus Santae Martae*, a public hotel and residence within Vatican City, as his *portiuncula*, rather than the papal palace? That, months into his papacy, he continues to wear a plastic wristwatch, his usual black shoes and trousers under his white papal cassock, and the pectoral cross of nonprecious metal that he had when in Buenos Aires? That, on his first Holy Thursday as pope, he stranded the thousands who had tickets for the planned papal ceremony in St. Peter's Basilica, not to mention some thirty cardinals expecting to attend, and chose instead to celebrate Mass at the Casal del Marmo, a Roman prison for adolescents, where he washed the feet of twelve prisoners, two of whom were women and two Muslims? Someone in the crowd at the prison asked, "Thank you, Father, for coming here today. But I want to know one thing: why did you come here to Casal del Marmo today?" The pope replied, "It was something that came from my heart. I just felt it. Where are those who perhaps could help me to be more humble, to be a servant as a bishop must be? Where are people who might like a visit? Thank you so much for your welcome. Pray for me and don't lose hope. Always go forward! Thanks a lot."

Bringing Hope to History

In St. Francis, too, hope was made real, hope entered history, especially via the saint's contagious care for the poor. St. Bonaventure, who, along with Thomas of Celano, was one of Francis's first biographers, summarized *il poverello*'s life and influence this way:

> He was poor and lowly, but the Most High God looked upon him with such condescension and kindness that he not only lifted him up in his need from the dust of a worldly life, but made him a practitioner, a leader and a herald of gospel perfection and set him up as a light for believers so that by bearing witness to the light he might prepare for the Lord a way of light and peace into the hearts of the faithful.[10]

Francis of Assisi exemplifies, in a preeminent manner, the beauty of the Christian faith and the joy that comes from believing in it. Its promise is nothing less than the hope of the world. A poem by Sophocles and translated by Seamus Heaney comes to mind. In it the poet speaks of "a further shore . . . reachable from here" and a time when "hope and history rhyme."[11] In St. Francis of Assisi hope and history actually did come together and, memorably ever after, did achieve rhyme.

TWO

"My House Is Falling Down"

A recent profile of the manager of the New York Yankees, Joe Girardi, may serve as an illustration of the challenge the Church faces today. Girardi's family immigrated to the United States from the region around Torino, Italy. In college he met the woman he eventually married, an evangelical Christian. She convinced him that baseball should be his career. Girardi said, "She made me realize that I was playing because God gave me a gift and I would be able to share God's good news through my gift and talent." The interview continues:

> Although Girardi was brought up Catholic, he told me, "The Catholic Church, it seemed to me, growing up, was a lot of rules. You sit, you stand, you kneel; you sit, you stand, you kneel." He said, "[my wife] Kim introduced me to Jesus." He once described the moment to a reporter: "We were sitting in the basement of the Tri Delta sorority house. Kim explained salvation to me, and I silently prayed to receive Jesus as my Savior."[1]

Contrary to many misconceptions, this "personal" faith is not unique to evangelical Christianity. In his first encyclical letter, *Lumen Fidei* (*The Light of Faith*), a collaboration with Pope Benedict XVI, Pope Francis speaks of Abraham, "our father in faith," as one to whom God speaks, to whom God "reveals himself as a God who speaks and calls his name." The pope continues:

> Faith is linked to hearing. Abraham does not see God but hears his voice. Faith thus takes on a personal aspect. God is not the god of a particular place, or a deity linked to a specific sacred time, but the God of a person. . . . Faith is our response to a word that engages us personally, to a "Thou" who calls us by name.[2]

God's house, the Church, begins to fall down when its members do not hear themselves personally summoned to faith. Faith is eminently personal. Although others can intercede in our behalf, no one else can have faith for us. Nominal Church membership is not enough.

"I know in whom I have placed my trust," Cardinal Avery Dulles professed at the end of his life, echoing St. Paul. "Jesus Christ, the way, the truth and the life" (Jn 14:6). In St. Paul's words, "As God is faithful, our word to you is not 'yes' and 'no.' For the Son of God, Jesus Christ, who was proclaimed to you by us, Silvanus and Timothy and me, was not 'yes' and 'no,' but 'yes' has been in him" (2 Cor 1:18–20).

RECOGNIZING THE SIGNS OF THE TIMES

When we read in the conclusion of the Gospel According to St. Matthew that Jesus sends forth his disciples with the commission, "Go, therefore, make disciples of all the nations" (Mt 28:19), it appears that throughout its history the Church will be in a mode of endless expansion. The

Acts of the Apostles ends with Peter and Paul in Rome, "the ends of the earth." The expectation is raised, however, that such expansion will continue until the end of time. But as we now know, and at this present time in particular, the history of the Church contains a pattern of growth, decline, decay, and renewal, a pattern that unfolds not just once but over and over again.

From its very beginning the Church seemed unlikely to last. This alarming thought was casually pointed out to me by Count Enrico Galeazzi (1896–1986), former governor of Vatican City and later official architect of St. Peter's Basilica in Rome. A close confidante of Pope Pius XII up until the pope's death, Galeazzi made this comment while giving me a personal tour of the excavations under the basilica. Amazingly, until the 1940s, when the excavations were undertaken, no one seemed interested in exploring the actual site of St. Peter's burial, although the location of which was the very reason that the Emperor Constantine erected the original basilica in this particular place. The Renaissance masters who produced the modern St. Peter's, Galeazzi explained, were less interested in archeology than in the extraordinary opportunity they were given to display their own talents.

As we made our way among the giant columns from the time of Constantine, which lay on the ground like trees fallen in a giant forest, he pointed out that nearly three hundred years had elapsed between the martyrdom of St. Peter and the erection of the first basilica, which required the desecration of an ancient cemetery on the Vatican hill across the Tiber from Rome's center. The apostle Peter had been simply buried in the cemetery nearest to the Circus of Nero where he been martyred. Constantine had the tops of mausoleums chopped off and filled with dirt to make the foundations of his new building. Before that, Peter's grave was just one among many others and remained so for hundreds of years, a remnant of a sect that worshipped as divine a man who died in a remote province of the Roman Empire. We gain a better sense of this time period if we remember that the time between Peter's death and the erection of the basilica was longer than the time between the Declaration of Independence and today.

The general disillusion in the West after the upheaval of World War II resulted in a new resurgence of Catholicism. Vocations to the priesthood and religious life were on the upswing. The Second Vatican Council convoked by Blessed John XXIII in 1962 captured this moment of renewal and reform.

In his homily commemorating the fiftieth anniversary of the Second Vatican Council, Pope Benedict XVI said that the challenge of a religious renewal fifty years later is no less urgent but even more difficult, because, he said, of the growing spiritual "desertification" of contemporary life. Ours is a culture of noise and of lies.

The world St. Francis of Assisi was born into, on a smaller scale certainly, bore all the marks and the wounds of a militaristic and commercial culture like ours. The old feudal stratification of society was beginning to be altered by persons such as Francis's own father, a dealer in expensive cloth whose work required regular business trips to the Champagne region of France. Pietro Bernadone is described by a scholar learned in the history of the period as "dominated solely by the instinct of money, a master of swindle only interested in increasing his business, in setting traps, haughty, sometimes treacherous, even violent."[3]

Upon learning on his return from one of his trips to France that his wife had their son christened "Giovanni," he replaced the name with Francesco, "the little French one," expressing his admiration for all things French. Francesco learned to speak rudimentary French and loved to sing French ballads. He certainly absorbed his father's way of life and that of the city of Assisi, which was perpetually at war with Perugia and other neighboring places, not to mention the Holy Roman Empire.

Splendidly covered with the gear of a knight, Francesco was captured by the Perugians, and during his capture he contracted tuberculosis. Since up until this point in his life he had been the center of entertainment and fun, Francesco began to become disillusioned with his former ideals of chivalry. He began to change. Back in his father's business, he once shooed out a beggar for disturbing the customers. Ashamed of himself, he pursued the beggar to give him some alms.

When Francis was dying and dictating his testament, he recalled how an encounter with a leper at about the same time had transformed him:

> This is how God inspired me, Brother Francis, to embark upon a life of penance. When I was in sin, the sight of lepers nauseated me beyond measure, but then God himself led me into their company and I had pity on them. When I had once become acquainted with them, what had previously nauseated me became a source of spiritual and physical consolation for me. After that I did not wait long before leaving the world.[4]

In school Francesco would have heard about the legends of St. Martin of Tours of France (315–399), a military man who, upon encountering a beggar, dismounted his horse and cut his own cloak in half to clothe him.

In the year 1207, Francesco absented himself from work and turned to a life of prayer in the ruined chapel of San Damiano. It was there that something decisive happened. From the crucifix, Christ spoke to him and said, "Francis, repair my house for it is falling down." At first he thought he was being charged with restoring this old church building. For this purpose he stole a bolt of expensive cloth from his father's store and sold it to help the restoration. As his Franciscan biographer Thomas of Celano observed, "Francis was an excellent craftsman, according to whose form, rule and teaching the church itself is renewed."[5] Celano continues,

> And thus Francis undertook his first work having obtained freedom from the carnal hand of his father. He constructed a house for God, and did not try to build it *de novo*, but he repaired the old one, he restored an ancient one. He did not tear out the foundation but built upon it, reserving that prerogative, though he did not know it, for Christ. "For one can lay no other foundation except that one which has already been laid, which is Jesus Christ" (1 Cor 3:11).[6]

Pietro Bernadone was not pleased with his son's actions. After having confined him to quarters but still unable to change Francesco's mind, the father brought his son to trial before the bishop and the town council. The day was snowy and cold. The bishop sided with the father and demanded the restoration of the stolen money.

Francis returned the gold, but did something more. He stripped himself naked, giving back to his father the expensive clothes he was wearing. "Up until today," he said, "I have called Pietro Bernadone my father. For the future I shall say, 'Our Father who art in heaven.'"[7]

This dramatic gesture had even more implications. Modern scholarship has uncovered the fact that Francis's mother brought a substantial dowry to her marriage that might have funded her husband's business. Francis would have been entitled to a portion of the dowry upon her death. He also gave up that right when he left his father's house for good.

The people of Assisi at first shared the embarrassment that this once-promising youth was now a beggar dressed in rags. Over the course of time, however, the townsfolk recognized Francis's sincerity and came to admire his evident piety. Some of the wealthy class even asked to join him in his life of voluntary poverty. As their number grew, Francis wished to receive Church approval for his new company. But first he needed a rule of life for them to follow. According to the belief of the time, if you opened a book of scripture randomly, the first verse that met your eyes was what God was asking you to hear. Francis went to the Church of San Nicolo and asked the priest to open the book of the gospels three times at random to let God decide the new rule of life. Each was perfect.

The first passage was Matthew 19:21. Jesus, speaking to the rich young man, declares, "If you wish to be perfect, go, sell your possessions, give the money to the poor and you will have treasure in heaven. Then come and follow me."

The priest then opened the gospel book a second time, to Luke 9:3. To the Twelve setting out to proclaim the Gospel, Jesus says, "Take nothing for the journey: neither staff nor backpack nor bread nor money, and do not bring a spare tunic."

The third passage was equally significant and determined the course Francis would follow for the rest of his life. In Matthew 16:24 Jesus tells his disciples, "If anyone wants to be a follower of mine, let him renounce himself, take up his cross and follow me."

As it happens, that very gospel book now resides in the Walters Art Museum in Baltimore, Maryland. I once asked to see it but was told I needed an appointment since it is kept in a protected environment.

Accompanied by those who had joined his way of life, Francis then made a pilgrimage to Rome to ask the pope to approve this new order in the Church. Innocent III was not impressed, it turns out, with the ragtag group of mendicants, and he initially dismissed them. That night, however, Innocent had a dream. He dreamt that his cathedral church in Rome, San Giovanni in Laterano, was beginning to collapse, but a young man appeared who held up its roof with his strength. Innocent surmised that that young man was the person he had met the previous day.

Cardinal Ugolino, who admired Francis, told the pope,

> If we refuse the request of this poor man as novel or too difficult, we must be on our guard lest we commit an offense against Christ's gospel. For if anyone says that there is something novel or irrational or impossible to observe in this man's desire to live according to the perfection of the gospel, he is guilty of blasphemy against Christ, the author of the gospel.[8]

Pope Innocent approved the new order, giving it his protection. Per their request, he allowed the friars to preach to the people wherever they went. And they did so, preaching in their own language, a practice which until then was unheard of.

Time to Wake Up

The Pew Forum on Religion and Public Life recently published a study of religious practice in the United States. Its results showed dramatic shifts downward among those who identify themselves with any particular Christian denomination, Protestant in particular. The basic finding is that one in five adults has no religious affiliation, and that this percentage reaches its highest point among young adults. The Catholic share of the population has held steady due largely to the influx of Hispanics. Another significant part of the survey is that most of the population, nearly 70 percent, say they do believe in God and consider themselves religious or spiritual persons.

Peter Steinfels, in a column in *Commonweal* magazine titled "Further Adrift," claims that if ex-Catholics would form a single church, that church would be the second largest denomination in the United States. Many inside the Church have recognized for some time the challenges posed by Steinfel's observed facts. In July 1978 the renowned Jesuit biblical scholar Carlo Martini was named rector of the Gregorian University in Rome. A little more than a year later, Pope John Paul II named him archbishop of Milan, the world's largest diocese with five million inhabitants. It might have seemed odd for the pope to name a professor to such a post, but what the pope seemed to be signaling was that the Church was more in need of effective teachers than administrators.

At the time I was among the other rectors of seminaries in Rome who met with Archbishop Martini before his departure for Milan. A tall, shy man, I remember his saying to us that he had no fears about assuming this awesome responsibility because the archdiocese was well organized, and so he intended to spend his time preaching the Gospel to all age groups—which indeed he did, holding, for example, Sunday afternoon catechetical sessions with youth in the cathedral. Quoting the Letter to the Hebrews, he said that those who have heavy responsibilities in the Church should bear them lightly because otherwise they become a burden to their flock.

Cardinal Martini died on August 31, 2012. Before his death he gave an interview in which he said that the Church is two hundred years out of date in terms of presenting its message effectively. He said, in part:

> The Church is tired in affluent Europe and America. Our culture has grown old, our churches are empty, the bureaucracy of our churches is growing out of proportion, our liturgies are pompous. . . . How is it that the Church does not rouse itself? Are we afraid? Fearful instead of courageous?[9]

To remedy this decline, some had called for a smaller, purer Church, a saving remnant, a mustard seed. Accordingly, they argued that the Church must purge herself of the semipagans who, though baptized, have adopted the values of the prevailing culture. This was, of course, the same line adopted in the time of St. Augustine, when many Catholics defected because of the persecution the Church was enduring. The people taking this position of expelling the weak were called the Donatists, and they were regarded as heretics by Augustine. The Church, Augustine contended, must remain Catholic, open to all, leaving to God at the end of time to sort out the wheat from the chaff, the saints from the sinners.

The inauguration of the papal ministry of Pope Francis took place on the Feast of St. Joseph, patron of the universal Church. Pope Francis developed the theme of Joseph as protector, in the first place of Jesus and Mary and then, by extension, of the Church itself. During his homily on Joseph's feast, the new pope looked to Joseph as a model of how to rebuild the Church in our time:

> How does Joseph respond to his calling to be the protector of Mary, Jesus and the Church? By being constantly attentive to God, open to the signs of God's presence and receptive to God's plans, and not simply to his own. This is what God asked of David, as we heard in the first reading. God does not want a house built by men, but faithfulness to his word, to his plan. It is God himself who builds the house, but from living stones sealed by his Spirit. Joseph is a "protector" because he is able to hear God's voice and be guided by his will; and for this reason he is all the more sensitive to the persons entrusted to his safekeeping. He can look at things realistically, he is in touch with his surroundings, he can make truly wise decisions. In him, dear friends, we learn how to respond to God's call, readily and willingly, but we also see the core of the Christian vocation, which is Christ! Let us protect Christ in our lives, so that we can protect others, so that we can protect creation![10]

THREE

"THE DRAGON IS IN CHARGE OF THE CITY"

A recent book by child psychologist Madeline Levine reveals patterns of modern parenting that are disturbing. According to the author, the version of success parents are promoting to their children leaves them "trauma victims." She writes, "Kids laugh when I tell them parents don't mention money as a measure of success; they think I've been snowed." She finds these kids looking good on the outside and feeling rotten inside.[1]

The author truly believes parents today want to be good parents, but the culture we live in bases success on competition and materialism, with clear winners and losers. She offers an alternative vision of parenting meant to help children aim toward other kinds of goals: becoming capable of empathy toward others; striving to be their best selves, whoever that may be; and, finally, learning to dream.

Doesn't this inescapably bring to our minds the young dreamer Francis of Assisi, who by his teaching and example taught people another way to live their lives? Perhaps Levine is on to something. We can teach our children to dream, not of ever-expanding material comforts, but of, in Pope Francis's words, "a Church which is poor and for the poor!"

"*Uscii questo mondo*" ("I have left this kind of world") were the defiant words Francis of Assisi uttered in 1206 when he repudiated his father's values and embarked upon the path of voluntary poverty. "This kind of world" encompassed not only the deal-making culture of commercialism that was beginning to replace the feudal society of the Middle Ages but also the constant warfare and acceptance of violence that were simply part of life at that time. Francis himself had bought into it during his brief and disillusioning time as a knight in the military of Assisi fighting and losing to Perugia's forces.

Three years later, in 1209, Silvestro, a canon of Assisi's Cathedral of San Ruffino, had a vision. He saw Assisi encircled by a huge and ferocious dragon (Dn 14:22) that was frightened away by a single brave knight. That dragon was no myth. It represented in concrete form a powerful force embodying all the false values that hold people in their thrall. In scripture and in Christian literature about the saints and angels, that ominous, powerful threat is called "Satan," the *satanas*—the adversary and the accuser.

The twelfth chapter of the Book of Revelation depicts "a great sign" that appeared in the heavens: a woman about to give birth and crowned with stars, standing on the moon and clothed with the sun, menaced by a red dragon with seven heads with a crown on each of them. God comes to rescue the woman and her child, understood ever since to be Mary and Jesus. War breaks out, and it is the archangel Michael who appears and hurls the dragon down from the sky. However, the dragon again springs back to life and makes war on those who obey God and God's commandments, those who witness to Jesus by their life.

According to his biographer Thomas of Celano, St. Francis of Assisi had a special veneration for angels as trusted allies in our struggles against evil. In particular, he counted upon St. Michael the archangel. Thus it was that in August of 1224, barely two years before his death and while already weak from ill health, Francis began an intense period of fasting and prayer to culminate forty days later at the Feast of St. Michael. He chose as its location La Verna, a mountainous region of trees, exceptional views, and birds. It had been given to his religious order by a wealthy admirer and, by exception, he had accepted. On his way there, helped by the friars because of his poor health, Francis was approached by a local man. "Are you Francis of Assisi?" he inquired. When Francis affirmed this, the man said to Francis, "Well then, try to be as good as you can because everyone has great faith in you. Don't let them down."

Not allowing his companions to join him during his fast and prayer except when summoned, Francis brought two questions to God, questions he hoped to have resolved during that time: who are you, my dear Lord, and what am I, your useless servant? It was then that the most extraordinary event of Francis's life occurred that would forever after define him. Jesus appeared to him as a six-winged seraph and impressed upon Francis's body his own wounds from the Cross, the stigmata. Francis became the embodied image of Jesus himself in the age-old conflict with the oppressive dragon.

The Dragon and the City Today

The existential dilemmas elicited by life in a materialistic, consumerist society such as ours are well portrayed in a recent sketch by the comedian Jerry Seinfeld. He stands contemplating a wall of drinks in a supermarket and is compelled to try to figure out: "Who am I? Where am I? And what do I want to be?"

The materialism today is apparent in many ways. We are appalled to hear a Junior Chamber of Commerce radio advertisement recommending a program for parents on how to help elementary-aged children learn to manage their money because "it is never too soon for them to learn how to keep up with the Joneses." More, we are told over and over again, is always "better."

The "Occupy Wall Street" movement fizzled even though it was addressing a troubling, blatant fact: wealth is increasingly concentrated in the hands of the powerful few, while poverty increases for the rest. It seems our fear of disorder and chaos works against such protests that are in favor of radical change. The anxiety and anger circulating in our society conjure images of fictional heroes such as Batman streaming through the night, his black cloak unfurling behind him as he brings to justice the forces of darkness that threaten Gotham City. Of course, Batman ejects a small segment of rich white men from their luxury apartments but then returns to a luxury apartment of his own. At this moment in New York City, the tallest residential tower in the world is under construction. Named One57 for its location on 57th Street, and taking Central Park as its carpet, it is a global billionaire's club, with each apartment on the top floor selling for $90 billion. The scale of wealth represented by this building is unheard of.

Predatory banks and hedge funds control the markets at their pleasure. Fines are paid, but the securities fraud continues as money is also being laundered for drug cartels.

While prolonged and unwanted wars continue abroad, each year more than thirty thousand citizens are killed by guns domestically. People in our country use their freedom to purchase 4.5 million firearms in a single year. It seems we have become inured to the wide-scale loss of life dramatized at Columbine High School, at the cinema in Aurora, Colorado, and, more recently, at the elementary school in Newtown, Connecticut, and the Boston Marathon. The numbers of military veterans suffering from post-traumatic stress syndrome continue to grow as treatment for them lags.

At present the United States spends more on defense-related weapons and soldiers than all the other nations of the world combined. Upon leaving office in 1961, President Dwight Eisenhower, the former five-star general, urged that our government guard against the acquisition of influence by what he called the "military-industrial complex." The infatuation with military power and its display around the world has only increased since then.

Sin is both personal and social. The atmosphere of sin, a whole culture, must be challenged if personal behavior is to change. If the society's—not just the individual's—values are false and oppressive, then the society itself must be exposed.

The Catechism of the Catholic Church describes social sin this way:

> Thus sin makes us accomplices of one another and causes concupiscence, violence and injustice to reign among us. Sins give rise to social situations and institutions that are contrary to the divine goodness.

"Structures of sin" are the expression and effect of personal sins. They lead their victims to do evil in their turn. In an analogous sense, they constitute "social sin."[2]

What is being called the "new evangelization" would be shallow and totally marginalized if it did not imitate St. Francis in directly addressing this new dragon menacing our city.

Pope Francis has not been afraid to name the devil as the largest threat we are facing. In his first unscripted homily to the cardinals who elected him, he cited Léon Bloy, a voluntarily impoverished French writer: "Whoever does not pray to God, prays to the devil." Pope Francis continued, "When one does not profess Jesus Christ, one professes the worldliness of the devil."

In a May 2013 address given to a group of new ambassadors at the Vatican, Pope Francis forcefully illuminated the human and spiritual costs of a culture based exclusively on money and consumerism:

> People have to struggle to live, and frequently, to live in an undignified way. One cause of the situation, in my opinion, is our relationship with money and our acceptance of its power over ourselves and our society. Consequently, the financial crisis that we are experiencing makes us forget that its ultimate origin is to be found in a profound human crisis. In the denial of the primacy of human beings! We have created new idols. The worship of the golden calf of old (Ex 32:15–34) has found a new and heartless image in the cult of money and the dictatorship of an economy which is faceless and lacking any human goal.[3]

Part four of Pope Francis's encyclical *Lumen Fidei* is titled, "God Prepares a City for Them." In this section he explores faith not just as a personal journey,

> but also as a process of building, the preparing of a place in which human beings can dwell together with one another. . . . The God who is himself reliable gives us a city that is reliable. Precisely because it is linked to love, the light of faith is concretely placed at the service of justice, love, and peace. . . . Faith is truly a good for everyone. It is a common good; its light does not simply brighten the interior of a church, nor does it solely serve to build an eternal city in the hereafter; it helps us build our societies in such a way that they can journey towards a future of hope.[4]

The light of faith illuminates the dignity of human beings and dims the dictatorial dragon that is our faceless economy, making room again for the city of God.

FOUR

"Preach the Gospel Always. If Necessary, Use Words"

One day in 1980, Archbishop Jean Jadot (1909–2009), a former apostolic delegate to the United States and at that time head of the Vatican secretariat for non-Christians, invited me to tour his offices. He explained that there were two formal meeting rooms, each appropriately decorated: one for Buddhists, the other for Muslims. In the course of our tour, he introduced me to a Japanese priest, and the archbishop invited him to share with me how he had become a Christian and a Catholic.

His story was fascinating. He and his family had survived the atomic-bomb attack on their native island of Nagasaki at the conclusion of World War II. Their home was completely destroyed. To provide some shelter for his family, he and his brother came across a ruined Catholic church and started to steal some of its bricks to bring back home. To their alarm, the Catholic priest appeared and asked what they were doing. Thoroughly frightened, they explained themselves. To their surprise, instead of threatening them with punishment, the priest told them, "Well then, take as many bricks as you need." He was the first Christian they had ever met, and "Take as many bricks as you need" was their first instruction toward Christianity.

The quotation in the chapter title has often been attributed to St. Francis, though *il poverello* may never have actually uttered these words. Whether he did or not, the ministry of preaching repentance and conversion to the Gospel way of life was for Francis deeply connected to intense personal prayer, the practice of penance, and the witness of charity in the life of the one who presumed to preach. Word and witness have to be one and the same. Sometimes Francis saw the duty of prayer as so paramount that he wondered whether he should take time from prayer to preach at all. It was only at the urging of Clare and the brothers that he continued to preach to the people the saving message. Francis's preaching had such power, and was so challenging to the demons of his time, *because* he prioritized prayer and embodied witness over preaching.

On one occasion Francis was ordered by the bishop to preach to Clare and the sisters at her convent. They, of course, regarded him as their supreme mentor and example, a living saint. How could he possibly fulfill such expectations? Francis raised his eyes to heaven, where his heart always was, and began to pray to Christ. He then commanded ashes to be brought to him, made a circle with them around himself on the pavement, and sprinkled the rest of them on his head. When they waited for him to begin and the blessed father remained standing in silence, no small astonishment arose in their hearts. The saint then suddenly arose and, to the amazement of the nuns, recited the *Miserere mei Deus* (Psalm 50) in place of a sermon. When he had finished, he quickly left. The servants of God were so filled with contrition because of the power of this symbolic sermon that their tears flowed in abundance and they could scarcely restrain their hands from inflicting punishment on themselves.[1]

Examples of Francis's preaching abound. I will include just two more. This first comes from St. Bonaventure's life of the saint:

> It happened once that he came to Arezzo at a time when the whole city was shaken by civil war and was on the brink of destruction. Given hospitality in the outskirts, he saw over the city devils rejoicing and inflaming the troubled citizens in mutual slaughter. In order to put to flight those seditious spiritual powers, he sent Brother Sylvester, a man of dove-like simplicity, before him like a herald, saying, "Go before the gate of the city and on the part of Almighty God command the devils to leave immediately!" This truly obedient man hastened to carry out his father's orders and, singing psalms of praise before the face of the Lord (Ps 94:2), he began to shout out forcefully before the gate of the city: "On the part of Almighty God and at the command of his servant Francis, depart far from here, all you devils." At once the city returned to peace and all the citizens reformed their civil statutes very peacefully. Once the raging pride of the devils, which had surrounded the city like a siege, had been driven out, the wisdom of a poor man, namely the humility of Francis, entered in, brought back peace and saved the city. By his lofty virtue of humble obedience, he had gained such powerful control over those rebellious and obstinate spirits that he could repress their ferocious brashness and drive back their savage violence.[2]

A second example occurred in the year 1222, on the Feast of the Assumption, when Francis gathered a crowd in the piazza of the university city of Bologna. Here is an eyewitness account of what happened:

> When I was a student in Bologna, I saw St. Francis preach in the main square outside the Palazzo Communale; almost the whole city had gathered to hear him. His theme was "Angels, Men and Devils."
>
> Although no scholar, he spoke so well and developed the subject of these three classes of rational and spiritual beings so clearly that he won the unbounded admiration of even the academics in the crowd. Yet it was more of a general address than a sermon.
>
> He wore a tattered habit, his appearance was insignificant and his face wasn't handsome, but God gave his words such power that they actually restored peace to many of the noble families long torn apart by hatred, cruelty and murder. At the same time ordinary men and women flocked to him out of devotion and respect, afterward trying to tear a shred from his habit or at least to touch him.[3]

BRINGING LIGHT TO TODAY'S DARKNESS

The homily Pope Francis gave in St. Peter's Basilica at the Holy Thursday Chrism Mass following his election conveyed a conception of the priesthood that is eminently Franciscan. A priest must be one who is willing to go out to the edges, the fringes of society, to the poor, the prisoners, and the sick, to whose who are sorrowing and alone. He must recognize that he is not anointed for himself but to anoint the people. Pope Francis explained:

A good priest can be recognized by the way his people are anointed. This is a clear test. When our people are anointed with the oil of gladness, it is obvious: for example, when they leave Mass looking as if they have heard good news. Our people like to hear the gospel preached with unction; they like it when the gospel we preach touches their daily lives, when it runs down like the oil of Aaron to the edges of reality, when it brings light to moments of extreme darkness, to the "outskirts" where people of faith are most exposed to the onslaught of those who want to tear down their faith. People thank us because they feel we have prayed over the realities of their everyday lives, their troubles, their joys, their burdens and their hopes. And when they feel that the fragrance of the anointed one, of Christ, has come to them through us, they feel encouraged to entrust to us everything they want to bring before the Lord: "Pray for me, Father, because I have this problem," "Bless me," "Pray for me."[4]

The pope went on to denounce in specific terms priests who have reduced their priesthood to the point that they have become mere managers or administrators, who do not feel the need to put their own hearts on the line, who become "antique collectors" instead of living with the smell of the sheep. No wonder such priests experience a crisis of identity![5]

The next day, Good Friday, at the end of the Stations of the Cross ceremony, Pope Francis addressed the central message of St. Francis of Assisi: the cross.

I do not wish to add too many words. One word should suffice this evening and that is the cross itself. The cross is the word through which God has responded to evil in the world. Sometimes it may seem as though God does not react to evil, as if he is silent. And yet God has spoken, he has replied, and his answer is the cross of Christ, a word which is love, mercy, forgiveness. It also reveals a judgment, namely that God, in judging us, loves us. . . . If I embrace his love then I am saved, if I refuse it, then I am condemned, not by him but by my own self, because God never condemns, he only loves and serves.[6]

While the keynote of the preaching of St. Francis and Pope Francis is the cross, the entire mood and effect of such preaching is a joy that comes from the renunciation of worldly goods and the freedom that such renunciation makes possible. St. Bonaventure describes how Francis, once freed from the burdens of wealth, first experienced perfect joy:

Released now from the chains of all earthly desires, this despiser of the world left the town and in a carefree mood sought out a hidden place of solitude where alone and in silence he could hear the secrets God would convey to him. While Francis, the man of God, was making his way through a certain forest, merrily singing praises to the Lord in the French language, robbers suddenly rushed upon him from an ambush. When they asked in a brutal way who he was, the man of God, filled with confidence, replied with these prophetic words: "I am the herald of the great King." But they struck him and hurled him into a ditch filled with snow, saying, "Lie there you hick herald of God!" When they went away, he jumped out of the ditch, and brimming with joy, in a loud voice began to make the forest resound with the praises of the Creator of all.[7]

This early experience of perfect joy is consistent with one of the *fioretti* from his life. The *fioretti*, or "little flowers," are anecdotes remembered from the life of the saint and written down about a hundred years later by Franciscan hermits and others who preserved them. In this one, Francis patiently explains to his companion Brother Leo the meaning of perfect joy.

> If when we shall arrive at St. Mary of the Angels, all drenched with rain and trembling with cold, all covered with mud and exhausted from hunger; if, when we knock at the convent-gate, the porter should come angrily and ask us who we are; if, after we have told him, "We are two of your brethren," he should answer angrily, "What you say is not the truth; you are but two imposters going about to deceive the world, and take away the alms of the poor; begone I say"; if then he refuse to open to us and leave us outside, exposed to the snow and rain, suffering from cold and hunger till nightfall—then, if we accept such injustice, such cruelty and such contempt with patience, without being ruffled or murmuring, believing with humility and charity that the porter really knows us, and that it is God who makes him speak thus against us, write down, O Brother Leo, that this is perfect joy.[8]

In his homily on Palm Sunday on March 24, 2013, in St. Peter's Square, Pope Francis described how Jesus that day entered Jerusalem. The Pope's emphasis was on that same perfect *joy*:

> Crowds, celebrating, praise, blessing, peace: joy fills the air. Jesus has awakened great hopes, especially in the hearts of the simple, the humble, the poor,

the forgotten, those who do not matter in the eyes of the world. He understands human sufferings, he has shown the face of God's mercy, and he has bent down to heal body and soul. . . .

And here the first word that I wish to say to you: joy! Do not be men and women of sadness: a Christian can never be sad! Never give way to discouragement! Ours is not a joy born of having many possessions, but from having encountered a Person, Jesus, in our midst; it is born from knowing that with him we are never alone, even at difficult moments, even when our life's journey comes up against problems and obstacles that seem insurmountable, and there are so many of them! And in this moment the enemy, the devil, comes, often disguised as an angel, and slyly speaks his word to us. Do not listen to him! Let us follow Jesus! We accompany, we follow Jesus, but above all we know that he accompanies us and carries us on his shoulders. This is our joy, this is the hope that we must bring to this world.[9]

THE PHENOMENON OF ST. PIO OF PIETRELCINA

In his recent book *Padre Pio: Miracles and Politics in a Secular Age*, Sergio Luzzatto tries to assess why this obscure Franciscan monk who never left the small town of San Giovanni Rotondo is perhaps the most popular Catholic saint of the twentieth century. For many years the Vatican tried to suppress St. Francis's influence, once sending an emissary who was totally puzzled about his magnetic attraction. In his report, the emissary mused,

How is it that a man who has no exceptional natural qualities, and who is anything but free of shadows and defects, has been able to build a popularity that has few equals in the religious history of our times? How does one explain the irresistible fascination exerted by this man of faith with a weary air about him, with rough manners and a disagreeable voice?[10]

Blessed John Paul II, who canonized Padre Pio, provided an answer to this query. As a seminarian he had journeyed to San Giovanni Rotondo to ask Padre Pio to hear his confession. He said that after that experience Padre Pio represented for him "the intimate link between death and resurrection that composes the mystery of Christ's return." Padre Pio's suffering body, which bore the stigmata of Christ for most of his life, was "like bread that had been broken for men hungry for God the Father's pardon."[11]

Padre Pio died in 1968. Before his death some of my classmates in the seminary in Rome went to attend his daily Mass, and we knelt in line afterward to receive his blessing. As he passed among them, Pio stopped in front of one of them and abruptly told him, "You will never be ordained a priest." He never was. There is no shortage of such profound stories associated with the man from Pietrelcina. Luzzatto comes to the conclusion that "Padre Pio's stigmata and his miracles interest us less for what they tell us about him than for what they tell us about the world around him. . . . Padre Pio's stigmata did not appear at just any moment."[12]

The slaughter of World War I created a need for some meaning in such terrible suffering and, as has always been the case throughout history, that meaning was best revealed as having its heart in the wounds of Christ. "The useless slaughter of that war," as Pope Emeritus Benedict XVI has described it, seemed to be the direct result of a secular modern society whose scientific knowledge was used to kill as many people as possible. St. Pio of Pietrelcina provides an example of how an obscure witness can impact the whole world by preaching a Gospel of repentance and conversion. Pope Francis, who emerged from relative obscurity to assume the shoes of Peter and boldly proclaim the kingdom of God and the call to repentance, further demonstrates this divine logic.

THE EVANGELIZING MISSION TODAY

In its final propositions the Synod on the New Evangelization described four elements which comprise the mission of every baptized person.

The first is the irreplaceable element of personal witness, which requires that we be willing to live the Gospel in all its novelty and challenge. This demands the courage of St. Francis, who tried to do literally what the Gospel requires.

Secondly, a true follower of Christ must strive toward perfect charity, loving God above all and our neighbor as ourselves, as Jesus taught when he summarized all the law and the prophets (Mt 22:36–40). The obvious care and love the first Christians practiced among themselves, and toward many others besides, attracted many people to this new way; we read in the Acts of the Apostles that "they were looked up to by everyone" (Acts 2:46).

The third element of evangelization is transforming the place where one lives and the sphere in which one has influence as a Christian. We must be Christ's salt and light if the earth is to be transformed according to the vision of the kingdom of God.

Finally, the Christian must not shirk from the duty to directly and boldly invite others to know Jesus Christ. Today this duty oftentimes means that we must share the Gospel with members of our own families.

The first little brothers of St. Francis had an enormous initial impact upon the people because they preached to them in their own language, a novel phenomenon. The Mass, of course, was not in their own language, and the priests rarely preached at Mass, mostly because they were ill equipped to do so; seminaries for the training of priests would come centuries later. The power of evangelical preaching, as demonstrated by those friars, cannot be over estimated. The scriptures themselves were not merely "inspired" by God when they were written but are also "inspiring" today in their power to touch the hearts of all who hear them preached.

Before the Second Vatican Council, many believed—and in the East many continue to believe—that only monks are perfect Christians. The Council taught that all the baptized are called to one and the same perfection but by different paths. Further, *all* the baptized—not just priests, deacons, nuns, and brothers—are called to be evangelists.

PART TWO

REBUILDING THE CHURCH

FIVE

THE GOSPEL WAY OF LIFE:
PRAYER, PENANCE,
AND CHARITY

This chapter and the ones that follow highlight specifically Franciscan elements for the Church's renewal in our day. Personal witness through the practice of prayer and self-denial are key, as well as maintaining a conscious connection with those on the fringes of society whom we call the poor. Care for creation and the pursuit of peace among all the diverse people and religions of the world are also part of this vision.

But underlying each of them is the act of keeping front and center the Cross of Christ, the "sign of contradiction," the very symbol of Christ's self-giving love by which our redemption is accomplished. Recall what Pope Francis said to the cardinals who had just elected him pope: "When we walk without the cross, when we build without the cross, and when we profess Christ without the cross, we are not disciples of the Lord."

In his retelling of the life of holy Francis, his follower St. Bonaventure describes how Francis took his first steps of conversion to the Gospel way of life:

After that he began to seek out solitary places, well suited for sorrow; and there he prayed incessantly with unutterable groanings (Rm 8:26). After long and urgent prayer, he merited to be heard by the Lord. One day while he was praying in such a secluded spot and became totally absorbed in God through his extreme fervor, Jesus Christ appeared to him fastened to the cross. Francis's soul melted (Cant 5:6) at the sight, and the memory of Christ's passion was so impressed on the innermost recesses of his heart that from that hour, whenever Christ's crucifixion came to his mind, he could scarcely contain his tears and sighs, as he later revealed to his companions when he was approaching the end of his life. Through this the man of God understood as addressed to himself the Gospel text: If you wish to come after me, deny yourself and take up your cross and follow me (Mt 16:24).[1]

Embracing the Cross of Christ is the central key of Franciscan spirituality. The cross is the road to charity and the source of peace and joy. While these latter are also characteristics of Franciscan spirituality, and perhaps they are those attributes most commonly connected with Franciscans, the cross comes first. It is the necessary self-emptying following the example of Christ himself. The cross then, of necessity and in fidelity to the Gospel itself, must be the focus of preaching and of evangelization. Embracing the cross in all the actual circumstances of our lives is how we interpret our existence in this fallen world and how we experience its power to save us.

This is the way St. Francis himself expressed it:

[I]n preaching we must think, see, say and hear human things, adapting ourselves to them as if we were living on a human level, for men among men. But there is one thing to the contrary, that seems to outweigh all these considerations before God, namely that the only begotten Son of God, who in the highest wisdom, came down from the bosom of the Father, for the sake of souls. . . . [He came] to instruct the world with his example and to speak the word of salvation to men, whom he would redeem with the price of his sacred blood, cleanse with its washing and nourish with its draught, holding back for himself absolutely nothing that he could freely give for our salvation.[2]

St. Paul, in his fervent autobiographical outburst in the Letter to the Galatians, describes the process of embracing the cross:

> I have been crucified with Christ and yet I am alive; yet it is no longer I, but Christ living in me. The life that I am now living, subject to the limitation of human nature, I am living in faith, faith in the Son of God who loved me and gave himself for me. (Gal 2:20–21)

Having established his own "crucifixion," Paul moves from the particular to the general, enunciating the fact that *all* Christians must become familiar with the cross.

> All who belong to Christ Jesus have crucified self with all its passions and its desires. . . . After this, let no one trouble me; I carry branded on my body the marks of Jesus. (Gal 5:24; 6:17)

Conversion, as Pope Benedict XVI said, means passing from the "I" to the "Not-I," becoming a new self after the model of Christ. This often-painful, transformative purification involves a true dying to the previous way of life so that another may take its place. The imperial "I," with all its relentless desires and demands, has to be dethroned. Jesus declared in the Beatitudes, "Blessed are the pure of heart, for they shall see God" (Mt 5:8). Commenting on this saying, Søren Kierkegaard wrote, "Purity of heart is to will one thing." The heart that is divided, that cannot make up its mind, cannot see God.

In the Letter to the Philippians St. Paul admonishes believers to "make your own the mind of Christ Jesus." He explains this "mind" in the following hymn:

> Christ Jesus who, though he was in the form
>   of God,
> did not regard equality with God
> something to be grasped.
>
> Rather, he emptied himself,
> taking the form of a slave,
> coming in human likeness;
> and found human in appearance,
> he humbled himself,
> becoming obedient to death, even death on a
>   cross.
>
> Because of this, God greatly exalted him
> and bestowed on him the name
> that is above every name,
> that at the name of Jesus
> every knee should bend,
> of those in heaven and on earth
> and under the earth
> and every tongue confess that
> Jesus Christ is Lord,
> to the glory of God the Father. (Phil 2:6–11)

Conversion requires nothing less than "emptying your-self" of the self. This emptying, *kenosis* in the original Greek of St. Paul, means to pare away the lies and artificiality of the world in which we live and were brought up—to put these things away until we are able to experience the ultimate bareness of our existence. Only then do we come to realize that only God can redeem. As Wallace Stevens notes in his famous poem "The Snowman," it is to know "the mind of winter."[3]

The process of experiencing our emptiness before God is the way of the cross, the paschal mystery. It is passing over with Christ from this world to the Father.

There is no way to exaggerate how much the cross meant to St. Francis. Two contemporary prayers, which follow, that he knew in his lifetime and often prayed himself have survived and communicate to us over the centuries the personal meaning of the cross to the people of his time.

Prayer Before the Crucifix

Behold, O good and sweetest Jesus, I cast myself upon my knees in Thy sight, and with the most fervent desire of my soul I pray and beseech Thee to impress upon my heart lively sentiments of faith, hope and charity, true repentance for my sins and a most firm purpose of amendment: whilst with deep affection and grief of soul I consider within myself and mentally contemplate Thy five most precious wounds, having before my eyes that which David, the prophet, long ago spoke in Thy own person concerning Thee,

my Jesus: They have pierced my hands and my feet;
they have numbered all my bones.

ANIMA CHRISTI

Soul of Christ, sanctify me.
Body of Christ, save me.
Blood of Christ, inebriate me.
Water from the side of Christ, wash me.

Passion of Christ, strengthen me.
O good Jesus, hear me.
Within Thy wounds hide me.
Let me not be separated from Thee.

Defend me from the malignant enemy.
At the hour of my death call me:
And bid me to come to Thee,
That with Thy saints I may praise Thee
For all eternity.

In a typically powerful evangelical homily delivered on
the Second Sunday of Easter 2013 in the Lateran basilica—
the same basilica that Pope Innocent had dreamed was
collapsing until its roof was held up by a young man—Pope
Francis called our attention to the patience of God as God
awaits our conversion. He cited important biblical stories:
doubting Thomas "who wants to see, to put his hand in the
place of the nails and in Jesus' side; Peter's three-fold de-
nial; and the sad, despairing disciples on their way to Em-
maus on their 'barren journey' Easter Sunday." The pope
went on:

But Jesus does not abandon them: he walks beside them, and not only that! Patiently, he explains the scriptures that spoke of him, and he stays to share a meal with them. This is God's way of doing things: he is not impatient like us, who often want everything all at once, even in our dealings with other people. God is patient with us because he loves us, and those who love are able to understand, to hope, to inspire confidence; they do not give up, they do not burn bridges, they are able to forgive. Let us remember this in our lives as Christians: God always waits for us, even when we have left him behind!

I would like to emphasize one other thing: God's patience has to call forth in us the courage to return to him, however many mistakes and sins there may be in our life.[4]

We can obtain this increase in love, this necessary patience, by prayer, fasting and penance, and charity—these three pillars of Christian piety derived from Judaism and reaffirmed by Jesus in the Sermon on the Mount (Mt 6:1–18)—which find their exemplar in the life of the poor one of Assisi. These pillars must be the basis of any evangelization, old or new. Greater efforts need to be made to restore to the Church, for example, a more vigorous practice of fasting as an irreplaceable means both to experience our hunger for God (total fast, from all food and drink, for a limited time associated with the reception of the Eucharist) and to repair the effects of sin in our lives (partial fast for a more extended period as a penitential practice).

Contemporary Applications

It is hard if not impossible to be a Christian on one's own at any time in history, and especially in our own time. Society simply does not support such a commitment. This is why St. Francis assembled his community of friars: to live together what the Gospel teaches. It was an unconventional religious community in that it was not rooted in one place, but it was a group of itinerant preachers who nonetheless saw living in community as essential.

In our own day evangelization is taking place effectively through the new movements that have providentially sprung up in the Church. These movements help individuals receive the necessary support that large, sometimes anonymous, parishes cannot provide. It was Blessed John Paul II who once said that at its root the Church itself is a "movement."

The Cursillo ("little course" in Christianity) is a weekend experience that has brought many to Christ. It helps the conversion process through the intensity of its prayer and the personal witness of its leaders. The effects are often lifelong, since individuals recall the Cursillo retreat as the moment they met Christ for the first time even though they had been baptized Catholics at birth. Certain successors to Cursillo emphasize the renewal of entire parishes, so that the whole community can continue to guide and nourish its members in the Christian life. Whatever form it may take, a structured, intentional exposure to Jesus and his teachings can be life transforming.

The Rite of Christian Initiation of Adults (RCIA) is now an integral part of parish life. Instead of seeking admittance to the Church by simply meeting privately with the priest or catechist and becoming baptized, and then being cast adrift in the parish community, the candidate goes through various stages of conversion with the help and support of sponsors and the catechumenate community, a process in sync with the liturgical year. After the celebration at Easter of the sacraments of initiation, a period of "mystagogia" (reflecting on the sacramental mysteries already received) continues the personal integration into the life of grace.

The Neocatechumenal Way, like the Cursillo, began in Spain and is now a thriving, worldwide movement. It is called "neocatechumenal" because it is for Catholics already baptized, perhaps at birth, but never properly catechized. After the founders of this movement reached out to unaffiliated Catholics, they grew frustrated upon discovering the local parish communities were unable to receive and welcome them. They then brought a new, nurturing movement into being, a movement which in some ways operates parallel to the larger parish but with ties to it. I have visited seminaries sponsored by the Neocatechumenal Way in the United States. Their secret in promoting vocations is that they ask the community to select some of their members to consider this vocation—and it works! Some who never thought of becoming a priest are invited to do so and find a deep calling where they once heard nothing.

There are now many such movements in the Church. Opus Dei, founded by St. Josemaría Escrivá, has been prominent for many years and has a large membership that includes clergy as well as laity. Focolare and Comunione e Liberazione, both of which emerged from Italy after the Second World War, have a strong social mission. They are unmistakable signs of a new evangelization.

Today many parishes, and parish priests in particular, are obviously becoming overtaxed, so that even the welcoming of an evangelizing movement like the Neocatechumenal Way may seem little more than an added burden—in spite of the challenge of the new evangelization. Parishes have sometimes taken on the character of maintenance operations, providing services upon request. That is why Blessed John Paul II said, in endorsing the Neocatechumenal Way and other similar grassroots initiatives of the faithful, that perhaps the Church itself may best be defined as a "movement." He may also have given his approval because the anonymity of many large parishes leads many of their members to feel disconnected, even alienated. This is especially true when, in spite of their large sizes, parishes do not provide the nurturing support many people require to become and remain Christians in an often anti-Christian or secularized environment. We should keep in mind that the experience of being part of a community was very much integral to the birth of the Franciscan movement and its subsequent success.

The same tensions the Franciscan movement experienced with Church institutions continue today. But as history has shown, if successfully negotiated, the tensions can produce the renewal of those institutions.

Six

Love of God and God's Poor

At the end of his forty-day fast at La Verna, St. Francis experienced God in tongues of flame that burned into his body the very marks of Jesus' wounds. St. Bonaventure explains:

> Although his body was already weakened by the great austerity of his past life and his continual carrying of the Lord's cross, he was in no way terrified but was inspired even more vigorously to endure martyrdom. His unquenchable fire of love for the good Jesus had been fanned into such a blaze of flames that many waters could not quench so powerful a love.[1]

The philosopher Blaise Pascal (1623–1662), founder of modern mathematics and physics, described his conversion to Christ, when God personally revealed himself to him, using the image of flames. He recorded the precise date, November 23, 1654. He was in his thirties at the time and until then had shared the doubt and skepticism dominant during his time in history. For two hours the living God appeared to him, and he recorded the experience in a document that he kept ever after sewn into his clothing. It was discovered only after his death. This is what he wrote:

Fire
God of Abraham, God of Isaac, God of Jacob,
not of the philosophers and scientists.
Certitude, certitude, feeling joy, peace.
God of Jesus Christ.
"My God and your God" (Jn 20:17).
"Your God shall be my God" (Ru 1:11).
God is a consuming fire (Dt 4:24; Heb 12:29).
God speaks to Moses out of a bush on fire (Ex
     3:2).
God descends to give the Law on Sinai in
     sheets of flame (Ex 19:18).
The Holy Spirit descends in tongues of fire
     (Acts 2:3).

The tender love and acceptance manifested through the stigmata that Francis was given by Jesus must have had a deep imprint upon him given the rejection he experienced from his earthly father. Of course, Francis himself became a father to the religious community who gathered around him, and he displayed toward them all the qualities of the divine Father that he came to know. A fine example of this is how Francis was willing, out of fatherly concern, to set aside the rigors of fasting prescribed to the friars when one of them felt he was not up to it. Charity triumphed over fasting; as the Gospel teaches, mercy and love are greater than sacrifice. The incident is described by St. Bonaventure:

> Although he energetically urged the friars to lead an austere life, he was not pleased by an over-strict severity that did not put on a heart of compassion (Col 3:12) and was not seasoned with the salt of discretion. One night a friar was tormented with hunger because

of his excessive fasting and was unable to get any rest. When the devoted shepherd realized that danger threatened one of his sheep, he called the friar and put some bread before him. Then, to take away his embarrassment, Francis himself began to eat first and affectionately invited him to eat. The friar overcame his embarrassment and took the food, overjoyed that through the discreet condescension of his shepherd he had avoided harm to his body and received an edifying example of no small proportion. When morning came, the man of God called the friars together and told them what had happened during the night, adding this advice: "Brothers, in this incident let the charity and not the food be an example to you."[2]

On his deathbed St. Francis went back in his mind to a formative moment of his life, the time when, still in his father's employ, he met a leper begging for his help and he ran away from him in fear. His behavior, he recalled, shocked him. He asked himself: is this the kind of person I am?

The Lord gave me, Brother Francis, thus to begin doing penance in this way: for when I was in sin, it seemed too bitter for me to see lepers. And the Lord himself led me among them and I showed mercy to them. And when I left them, what had seemed bitter to me was turned into sweetness of soul and body.[3]

It was then that he began to learn charity in the model of Christ. With obvious admiration the disciple St. Bonaventure recalls the heights which Francis's charity achieved:

To beggars he wished to give not only his possessions but his very self. At times he took off his clothes, at times unstitched them, at times ripped them in pieces, in order to give them to beggars, when he had nothing else at hand. He came to the assistance of poor priests, reverently and devoutly, especially in adorning the altar. In this way he became a participator in the divine worship, while supplying the needs of its celebrants.[4]

By meditating on Jesus born in a stable, the incarnate Son of God, and Christ's suffering death upon a cross for the salvation of the world, Francis came to know the humility of God. If God can so humbly give himself toward us, why should we hold anything of ourselves back? In a letter to the entire fraternity Francis wrote these words:

> Look at the humility of God, and pour out your hearts before him! Humble yourselves that you may be exalted by him! Hold back nothing of yourselves for yourselves, that he who gives himself totally to you may receive you totally![5]

Even after he had received the stigmata and could barely walk because of his many illnesses—some brought on by his own extreme penances—he still continued to preach the Cross of Christ and love for the poor in the villages and towns. "Let us begin, brothers, to serve the Lord our God," he would say, "for up to now we have hardly progressed."[6]

CONTEMPORARY APPLICATIONS

When Pope Benedict XVI wrote the inaugural encyclical letter of his pontificate to the Christian people and to the world, he appropriately chose as its subject "God is Love." Drawing from this fundamental truth, the pope outlined what he termed the deepest nature of the Church in three indispensable duties: proclaiming and witnessing the Word of God; celebrating the sacraments; and exercising the ministry of charity. These three are translated from the Greek terms used in the New Testament: *kerygma-martyria*, *leitourgia*, and *diakonia*. "These duties presupposed each other and are inseparable," he said. And then the pope went on to make this startling claim:

> Worship itself, Eucharistic communion, includes the reality both of being loved and of loving others in turn. A Eucharist that does not pass over into the concrete practice of love is intrinsically fragmented.[7]

The holy sacrifice of the Mass must be made manifest in sacrificial service. Pope Benedict XVI's words carry forth Francis's insistence that we hold back nothing of ourselves for ourselves.

THE LOSS OF THE SABBATH

One of the most important means to practice the priority of God is the weekly observance of Sabbath. It is also a critical expression of the meaning of human life and of our dignity as sons and daughters of the Father, made in his own image and baptized as sisters and brothers of Christ.

All the religions of the world have festivals. What is unique about Judaism and subsequently Christianity is that a religious festival is celebrated every week. It was on the seventh day that God rested from the work of creation, and every Sabbath thereafter was to be a holy day of rest (Gn 2:1–3). The Sabbath also is intended to be a weekly reminder, by the prohibition against work on that day, of our personal dignity. Our value is not determined by the work we do and what we are able to produce and accomplish but by the fact that we are made in God's image (Gn 1:26). For Christians the weekly Sabbath rest is on Sunday, the first day of the week, the beginning of the new creation through Christ's resurrection from the dead.

Sadly, in our day the observance of Sabbath has practically passed out of existence. No one "has time" for it. As a result, one day blurs into another, every day the same. Celebratory family meals are rare. People snack and graze through the day; few have time to prepare meals. In a parish where I served as pastor, I asked every household to make a joint commitment to share a family meal together at least once a week. The meal was to begin by everyone at table expressing thanks for a blessing he or she had received and wished to share.

If the Sabbath's restoration is to be complete, it must include, as in the scriptures, everyone and everything, not just ourselves. All should have the opportunity on a regular basis to rest from their labors and to celebrate God's goodness. This encompasses our extended families, our coworkers, the poor, even the animals and the land itself.

Love of Others, Especially the Poor

In the context of the secularizing culture subsuming Europe and other First World countries, Pope Benedict XVI was right on when he chose to highlight the overwhelming, positive central message of Christianity and its power to transform individuals and society. He likewise demonstrated that, contrary to some of Christianity's most vocal critics, the Christian faith is not a narcissistic spirituality but a driving force for service to others.

Three years later, in 2009, the pope made his own contribution to the still-evolving social doctrine of the Church,
once again centering upon charity and its central truth and
impulse, in the encyclical *Charity in Truth*. "Love," Benedict XVI writes in the introduction, "is an extraordinary
force which leads people to opt for courageous and generous engagement in the field of justice and peace."[8] He
continues:

> Charity is at the heart of the Church's social doctrine.
> Every responsibility and every commitment spelled
> out by that doctrine is derived from charity which, ac-
> cording to the teaching of Jesus, is the synthesis of
> the entire Law (cf. Mt 22:36–40). It gives real sub-
> stance to the personal relationship with God and with
> neighbor; it is the principle not only of micro-rela-
> tionships with friends, with family members, within
> small groups, but also of macro-relationships, social,
> economic and political ones. For the Church, instruct-
> ed by the gospel, charity is everything because, as St.
> John teaches (Jn 4:8) and as I recalled in my first en-
> cyclical letter, "God is Love": everything has its origin
> in God's love, everything is shaped by it, everything is
> directed toward it.[9]

In one of this encyclical's most creative insights, the
pope introduces what he terms "the principle of gratuitousness." Our economic life will not serve the common
good unless we give recognition to the fact that most of
what we have and are is pure gift. He then urges that world
markets become more open to what he calls "forms of economic activity marked by quotas of gratuitousness and
communion."[10]

That last phrase, "quotas of gratuitousness," left many commentators scratching their heads. It is not a conventional economic term, to say the least. But what the pope is saying would be readily understood by St. Francis, who saw in nature itself a transcendent example of God's gifts to us. Nature, or "creation" as we usually describe it in religious terms, is not just the private domain of the human race, but it radically retains its relationship with God and its universal destination for the good of all God's creatures, human and nonhuman.

But the fundamental gift upon which human community is made possible is divine charity itself. This is why Pope Benedict says that the earthly city can be made to flourish only by relationships based upon gratuity, compassion, and mercy.[11] The human person is therefore "made for gift," which expresses and makes present this transcendent reality.[12]

Solidarity thus becomes a central ethical responsibility in society. Solidarity is defined as "first and foremost a sense of responsibility on the part of everyone for everyone."[13] Homeless persons are often simplistically described as lacking enough material goods to survive on their own, but, as Benedict reminds us, the greatest deprivation that poverty brings is the lack of human connections—the condition of being friendless.[14]

Beyond these basic truths, "quotas of gratuitousness" calls to mind newly emerging "mixed use" businesses that combine the profit motive with philanthropy and public service as part of their goals. But this gratuitousness is not possible merely on the level of macroeconomics. Every individual has his or her gift that he or she should be willing to share freely with others.

In my own community, to take just one example, there is an organization called "The Hour Exchange." It creates community bonds among people willing to share "time dollars." Their mission statement reads:

> We believe everyone has knowledge and skills that someone in the community can use. We help people find what they need and give what they can. We are neighbors helping neighbors help themselves. We are a community exchange service. If you give an hour of your time helping someone, providing a service, then you can receive an hour of someone else's time that provides a service you need. We are a community currency based on time.[15]

Even in a less economically developed time than our own, St. Francis and the friars were able to present and exemplify a new model of life in fraternity that was based not upon competition for scarce resources but on a mutual sharing of gifts. Community, friendship, and mutual sharing are still and will always be means by which we can meet basic human needs. The new evangelization can reshape the Church itself into such communities of mutual love.

According to St. Francis, the practice of personal poverty is how we can imitate in our own way of the Son of God, who impoverished himself to be born in Bethlehem of the Virgin Mary. Though he was divine, he became one like us. Jesus was a poor man who lived on alms given by others. He lived among the poor and marginalized. To practice such poverty is the way to encounter Jesus.

It has been said of Cardinal Bergoglio that, as evinced during his ministry in Buenos Aires before becoming pope, "he doesn't see the poor as people he can help but as people from whom he can learn. He believes the poor are closer to God than the rest of us; they have a very personal experience of him."[16]

THE TESTIMONY OF AVERY DULLES, S.J. (1918–2008)

Avery Dulles, son of the Secretary of State John Foster Dulles, was the foremost American theologian in the period after the Second Vatican Council. Created a cardinal by Blessed John Paul II, he lived through a period when some other theologians were espousing what was called "liberation theology" and asserting that the credibility of the Church's message today lies in its commitment to social justice. Dulles was not against social justice, but he believed that the credibility and ultimate attraction of Christianity was not to be found in anything we do but in the very person of Christ.

Avery Dulles grew up in a staunch Presbyterian household, but as a young man he drifted away from these beliefs. He confessed that God was unreal to him until something happened to him one winter evening when he was a junior at Harvard University, which he had selected over Princeton, his family's choice. He wrote of the experience in the book *A Testimonial to Grace*. He had been studying in Widener Library and, on impulse, decided to take some air. He walked along the banks of the Charles River toward Boston. The ground was muddy and covered with slush. At one point he looked up at a young tree, its branches just beginning to show buds. Spring was coming, and the tree, he realized, was following a rule, a law he had been previously unaware of. There must be an intelligence, a personal power that was guiding everything. That night, for the first time in years, he prayed.

> I knelt down in the chill blackness at my bedside, as my mother had taught me to do when I was a little boy, and attempted to raise my heart and mind toward him of whose presence and power I had become so unexpectedly aware. I recited the Our Father. The words came slowly, and I had to make many new starts before the whole prayer unfolded itself in my mind. Our Father who are in heaven. Hallowed by thy name. Thy will be done on earth, as it is in heaven."[17]

As a first-year law student at Harvard, Dulles was received into the Catholic Church. He later entered the Society of Jesus and was sent to Rome to do his doctoral work in theology, which is where I met him and where we began our friendship. In fact, in *A Testimonial to Grace* he mentions that when he returned home from Rome to begin his teaching career he was sent the class notes of a course in fundamental theology being taught by a new professor at the Gregorian, Rene Latourelle, S.J.[18] I was the one who sent him those notes.

Latourelle's work was important, not only to Dulles in his own development of the theology of divine revelation, but also in laying the groundwork for the Second Vatican Council's *Constitution on Divine Revelation* (*Dei Verbum*). In contrast with previous explanations of revelation as a series of propositions to be accepted and believed, the council taught that in divine revelation God actually "chose to show forth and communicate himself," sharing "treasures which totally transcend the understanding of the human mind."[19]

The postconciliar period in the Church was often tumultuous, especially for a theologian who approached theology not as a campaign for certain personal views but as a craft, for one who drew upon the ancient traditions and contemporary Church teaching authority. Avery once confided to me that he thought of giving up theology altogether: "I guess I'm not good at it," he said. But the fundamental conviction that sustained him he had already expressed in *Testimonial to Grace*:

> I came into the church like one of those timid swimmers who closes his eyes as he jumps into the roaring sea. The waters of faith, I have since found, are marvelously buoyant. Indeed, when man is clothed with grace, the sea of faith is his natural element.[20]

Upon being made a cardinal, Avery Dulles selected for his coat of arms these words of scripture: *"Scio cui credidi"* ["I know the one in whom I have placed my trust" (2 Tm 1:12)].

Dulles came to the Catholic faith as an adult and in the aftermath of World War II. Like so many others, having experienced personally the disillusionment with human enterprises to solve the world's problems, he placed his ultimate trust in Christ alone.

SEVEN

LOVE OF POVERTY
IN IMITATION OF JESUS

Early on in the itinerary of his conversion, St. Francis had a life-shaping encounter with Jesus upon the Cross, during which he heard words of Jesus addressed personally to him: "If you wish to come after me, deny yourself and take up your cross and follow me" (Mt 16:24). According to St. Bonaventure's official account of the order's holy founder, from that moment on, for the rest of his life, "whenever Christ's crucifixion came to his mind, he could scarcely contain his tears and sighs."[1] For Francis, a life of voluntary poverty was a necessary part of carrying Jesus' cross and denying himself. For Francis, the Lord Jesus Christ was truly born in poverty, lived in poverty, taught poverty, and died in poverty.

Bonaventure tells us that later on, Francis began to attract followers who needed some kind of holy rule to guide their life together. When Francis was devoutly hearing a Mass of the apostles, the Gospel was read in which Christ sends forth his disciples to preach and explains to them the way of life according to the gospel: that they should not keep gold or silver or money in their belts, nor have a wallet for their journey, not two tunics, not shoes nor staff (Mt 10:9). When he heard this, he grasped its meaning and committed it to memory. This lover of apostolic poverty was then filled with indescribable joy and said, "This is what I want; this is what I long for with all my heart." He immediately took off his shoes from his feet, put aside his staff, cast away his wallet and money as if accursed, was content with one tunic and exchanged his leather belt for a piece of rope. He directed all his heart's desire to carry out what he had heard and to conform in every way to the rule of right living given to the apostles.[2]

For Francis, becoming poor by choice is a condition for sharing in the choices of God's Son, entering Jesus' own world. Of course, voluntary poverty is a stunning counter-sign in a world based on the pursuit of wealth and its comforts. It is an implied call to conversion. But for Francis, voluntary poverty was above all learning the humility of God in very concrete fashion.

For the many whose poverty is not voluntary but rather their fate in life, and especially for those who live not in poverty but in *destitution*, we are called to share with them all the love that Christ brings to alleviate their sufferings.

The shoeless friars went about preaching the Gospel and supporting themselves with their own hands and by begging. They never wandered away from this holy ideal. But it was a struggle. This struggle was shared by Clare and her fellow sisters at the convent of San Damiano, who in their own way were following the evangelical life of poverty. Clare had also come from a wealthy family and defied their expectations to marry. She became enthralled with the example of her fellow townsperson Francis and secretly met with him, finally running away from home to the very convent of San Damiano. When her family pursued her there, they discovered that Francis had cut off Clare's beautiful hair as a sign of her definitive acceptance of this new life she had chosen for herself.

As indicated earlier, at the end his life Francis liked to repeat to the friars, "Let us begin, brothers, to serve the Lord our God, for up to now we have hardly progressed."[3] Self-impoverishment is not something we can say we have done. It is a never-ending process.

When St. Paul was writing one of the first charity-appeal letters in the history of Christianity—his Second Letter to the Corinthians—he based his call to the consciences of his fellow Christians upon the poverty of Christ. He first cited the example of the poor Christians of Macedonia who were outstanding in their response to come to the aid of the struggling Christian community in Judea. But his basic argument was that Christ had made himself poor for our sakes:

> We urged Titus that, as he had already begun, he should also complete for you this gracious act also.
>
> Now as you excel in every respect, in faith, discourse, knowledge, all earnestness, and in the love we have for you, may you excel in this gracious act also.
>
> I say this not by way of command, but to test the genuineness of your love by your concern for others.
>
> For you know the gracious act of our Lord Jesus Christ, that for your sake he became poor although

he was rich, so that by his poverty you might become rich. (2 Cor 8:6–9)

In Paul's mind, as in the mind of Francis, the practice of voluntary poverty was inevitably linked with compassion toward the poor. It is highly significant that when Paul recounts his going to Jerusalem to seek credentials from the apostolic community for his ministry to the Gentiles, he recalls that "James and Cephas and John, who were reputed to be pillars, gave me and Barnabas their right hands in partnership, that we should go to the Gentiles and they to the circumcised. Only, we were to be mindful of the poor, which is the very thing I was eager to do" (Gal 2:9–10).

In some ways St. Francis never abandoned the ideals of chivalry he had embraced as a young man. He continued to see himself as something of a troubadour, with all the romantic ardor associated with it. His pursuit of Lady Poverty, as he called her, was out of his chivalrous concern that no one else would marry such an unattractive woman. In Francis's life story depicted along the walls of the great basilica where he now is entombed, we see among the paintings of Giotto Francis's espousal to Lady Poverty.

CONTEMPORARY APPLICATIONS

It must be remembered that to the people of Assisi, who over time grew in their estimation of Francesco Bernadone, he became known as *il poverello*, the little poor one. A definition of voluntary poverty might be: to have nothing, to wish for nothing, and yet to possess all things truly in the spirit of freedom. In time *il poverello* called not just Assisi but the whole Church back to practicing the Gospel message that we must reject worldly goods and store up treasure in heaven.

When the Roman Empire was collapsing and Christianity, by the decree of Constantine, became the new official religion, the Church had to struggle on a grand scale with the right use of money and wealth because people of wealth were now entering the Church. In his recent book *Through the Eye of a Needle: Wealth, the Fall of Rome, and the Making of Christianity in the West, 350–550 AD*, Peter Brown traces the influence of the novel Christian idea—that we can place treasure for ourselves in heaven by giving our wealth to the poor while we are on earth—upon society. This flow of wealth from earth to heaven is how we pass "through the eye of a needle."

Brown says he wrote this book to show that those who see this period of Christian history as a falling away from the radicalism of the Christian movement are misguided. He writes:

> Renunciation of wealth was not the only act on which the hand of God rested. Gifts to the poor, donations to the church, weekly offerings, offerings for the payment of vows: each and all joined heaven and earth in ways that were all more deeply installed in the consciousness of believers for not being exhaustively analyzed. The imagined course of wealth from earth to heaven through humdrum acts of pious giving was just as important to Christian believers as was the occasional act of renunciation among the few. Those who shied away from or who toned down the command of Jesus to the Rich Young Man were not mere shirkers. Rather, they had surrounded their use of wealth with a different imaginative charge from that of the advocates

of radical renunciation. This charge empowered their daily acts of kindness and generosity. It was from this rich imaginative humus, common both to the wealthy and to distinctly ordinary persons, that the wealth of the church sprang."[4]

Brown cites many personal examples of this, among them St. Ambrose of Milan, who became bishop of that imperial city in 374, the first wealthy aristocrat to hold that office in the West. He developed a sense of one Christian people made up of persons of diverse backgrounds, all caring for one another. Cohesion and solidarity became the hallmark of the Church and it took over from the senatorial class much of the welfare system for the poor.

The story of Jesus and the rich young man is given to us in Matthew's gospel.

> And now a man came to him and asked, "Master, what good deed must I do to possess eternal life?" Jesus said to him, "Why do you ask me about what is good? There is one alone who is good. But if you wish to enter into life, keep the commandments." He said, "Which ones?" Jesus replied, "These. You shall not kill. You shall not commit adultery. You shall not steal. You shall not give false witness. Honor your father and your mother. You shall love your neighbor as yourself." The young man said to him, "I have kept all these. What more do I need to do?" Jesus said, "If you wish to become perfect, go and sell your possessions and give the money to the poor, and you will have treasure in heaven; then come, follow me." But when the young man heard these words he went away sad, for he was a man of great wealth.

Then Jesus said to his disciples, "In truth I tell you, it is hard for someone rich to enter the kingdom of Heaven. Yes, I tell you again, it is easier for a camel to pass through the eye of a needle than for someone rich to enter the kingdom of Heaven." When the disciples heard this they were astonished. "Who can be saved, then?" they said. Jesus gazed at them, "By human resources," he told them, "this is impossible; for God, everything is possible." (Mt 19:16–26)

Notice the progression in this story. The fundamental phase of discipleship is following the commandments of Moses. The second phase for a Christian is living the life of the Beatitudes, among which the first is, "Blessed are the poor in spirit" (Mt 1:3). It is in Matthew's gospel that we find "poor in spirit"; Luke simply says, "Blessed are you who are poor" (Lk 6:20). Many scholars suggest that that Matthew's community was already struggling with what it meant to be poor and be a follower of Jesus.

The image of a camel passing through the eye of a needle is, of course, ridiculous, a bit of Semitic exaggeration that Jesus sometimes used for effect. Some commentators believe that there was an actual tiny gate in the walls of Jerusalem called by that name. In any case, Jesus is asserting an impossibility.

The parable of Lazarus and the rich man found in Luke is also compelling for its depiction of the disturbing degree to which wealth can divide:

There was a rich man who dressed in purple garments and fine linen and dined sumptuously each day. And lying at his door was a poor man named Lazarus, covered with sores, who would gladly have eaten his fill of the scraps that fell from the rich man's table. Dogs even used to come and lick his sores. When the poor man died, he was carried away by angels to the bosom of Abraham. The rich man also died and was buried, and from the netherworld, where he was in torment, he raised his eyes and saw Abraham far off and Lazarus at his side. And he cried out, "Father Abraham, have pity on me. Send Lazarus to dip the tip of his finger in water and cool my tongue, for I am suffering torment in these flames." Abraham replied, "My child, remember that you received what was good during your lifetime while Lazarus likewise received what was bad; but now he is comforted here, whereas you are tormented. Moreover, between us and you a great chasm is established to prevent anyone from crossing who might wish to go from our side to yours or from your side to ours." He said, "Then I beg you, father, send him to my father's house, for I have five brothers, so that he may warn them, lest they too come to this place of torment." But Abraham replied, "They have Moses and the prophets. Let them listen to them." He said, "Oh no, father Abraham, but if someone from the dead goes to them, they will repent." Then Abraham said, "If they will not listen to Moses and the prophets, neither will they be persuaded if someone should rise from the dead." (Lk 16:19–31)

Notice that the rich man is not given a personal name like the poor man Lazarus. He is just someone defined by his wealth: a rich man. The parable takes note of the rich man's clothing: purple outer garments, the most expensive color and usually reserved to royalty, and undergarments made of linen. Notice also that his problem is not primarily that he did not come to the aid of Lazarus; it is that he simply did not know he existed. The rich man lived behind a gate that his wealth built up around him, a gate at which the poor man Lazarus used to beg. Shockingly, even dogs displayed more sympathy toward Lazarus, licking his sores. Instead of using the customary napkins, between the courses of his magnificent daily feasts the rich man wiped his face with pieces of bread, the "scraps" from the table that Lazarus was longing to eat.

The ways in which the two men die, each of which is described by the sacred author, are highly significant. Upon dying Lazarus is carried by angels into Abraham's embrace; all that is said of the rich man is that he also died and was buried—no angels, no Abraham's bosom. In fact, the rich man finds himself in Hades, a very long way from paradise. In his torment, the rich man begs Abraham to dispatch Lazarus to help him in his pain. Pay attention to the fact that even in the next world the rich man feels he can order around people like Lazarus. Abraham explains that this is impossible; a great reversal has taken place and God has righted the wrongs of the earth. Even worse, that wall that wealth created between the rich man and Lazarus on earth has become eternal in the next world, with no passing back and forth. The gulf is too great, and it is now permanent.

As it draws to its conclusion, the parable then takes a surprising twist. It is no longer just about a certain anonymous rich man and a poor beggar; it is about you and me, the listeners. Abraham asserts that no warning from the next world to the brothers still left is necessary, for we, like them, "have Moses and the prophets" to listen to—and we had better listen! To the last desperate request of the rich man that Lazarus return from the dead to issue a warning, Abraham replies that if they will not listen either to Moses or to the prophets, whose writings and deeds are read in every synagogue every day, "they will not be convinced even if someone should rise from the dead"—as we know Jesus did.

The weekly Eucharist we attend proclaims God's word and allows us to be nourished with the bread of life. We should experience at every Eucharist in which we participate a new call to personal conversion through self-denial and service to the poor. As the dismissal in the new Roman Missal succinctly puts it: "The Mass is ended. Proclaim the Gospel by your life!"

The life of the first Christians as portrayed by Luke in the Acts of the Apostles has always been the standard and the challenge by which subsequent Christians have measured themselves. "All who believed were together and had all things in common; they would sell their property and possessions and divide them among all according to each one's need" (Acts 2:44–45). What are we to conclude for ourselves and for our Church today?

First, wealth can put its owners in the spiritually precarious position, imparting in them a false sense of independence from other human beings and even from God. Why do people want to set aside a nest egg for retirement if not to achieve this illusory "independence"? The poor have the spiritual advantage of knowing how dependent all of us are all the time upon God's benevolence.

Second, a joyful simplicity of life needs to be consciously cultivated. In a society based on consumerism, one artificially brought to higher and higher levels through advertising, this stance is definitely countercultural. The "domestic church," which is the home, should invite its members to mutual commitment to this ideal.

When Blessed John Paul II visited the United States in 1979 for the first time after his election as pope, he gave a homily in Yankee Stadium in New York City. Significantly, his exegesis was based upon Jesus' parable of Lazarus and the rich man (Lk 16:19–31). These are, in part, his applications:

Christians will want to be in the vanguard in favoring ways of life that decisively break with the frenzy of consumerism, exhausting and joyless. It is not a question of slowing down progress, for there is no human progress when everything conspires to give full reign to the instincts of self-interest, sex and power. We must find a simple way of living. It is not right that the standard of living of the rich countries would seek to maintain itself by draining of a great part of the reserves of energy and raw materials that are meant to serve the whole of humanity. For readiness to create a greater and more equitable solidarity between peoples is the first condition for peace. Catholics of the United States and all you citizens of the United States, you have such a tradition of spiritual generosity, industry, simplicity and sacrifice, you cannot fail to heed this call today for a new enthusiasm and a fresh determination. It is in the joyful simplicity of a life inspired by the gospel and the gospel's spirit of fraternal sharing that you will find the best remedy for our criticism, paralyzing doubt and the temptation to make money the principal means and indeed the very measure of human advancement.[5]

Third, wealth is an entrustment, not an entitlement. *To whom much has been given, much is expected. From each according to his or her ability, to each according to his or her need.* These are sound biblical aphorisms. In fact, the concept of "giving back" has been a very powerful motivating force for much good that is done in society all the time.

Fourth, everyone of every station in life has something to give. Time is a kind of money. Many give their time as volunteers. Some give a year or two of their lives in public service before entering into their own careers.

Some, in our time as in St. Francis's own lifetime, have the courage to leave all behind and follow him. From the earliest days of the Order of the Friars Minor, many came to accept that the world was full of vanity and greed and wished to follow Francis's teaching and example, but some did so by staying at home. These became the nucleus of a "third order" of Franciscans besides the religious orders of men and women. It was one of these people, for example, who offered St. Francis a beautiful track of land, La Verna, which Francis uncharacteristically accepted. The third order is now called the Order of Secular Franciscans, and they follow a rule of life based upon Franciscan spirituality.

The question of how much to give has always been an issue, even for Franciscans. I cite the following self-evaluation of a contemporary Franciscan:

> For example, if I begin exploring the parameters of what I do and am as a Franciscan in the light of who I'm supposed to be and how I'm expected to act, I see that my own living of the charism of St. Francis has shrunk to shocking proportions. The moorings of my Franciscan vocation, gospel poverty, fraternity, itinerancy, are exposed for what they've become in my life.

Poverty is now selective "giving up" of this or that minor materiality while my whole life is really lived out in a comfortable mediocrity. I am in the middle, as it were, straddling the fence between holiness and sinfulness. Straddling may be too strong an image for the comfortable, secure middle way I live. Fraternity has become a nominal, loose allegiance to my brothers, and itinerancy has become freedom to travel, sometimes where only those of independent means can go.

A rather harsh assessment of my life! I see that I have slipped quite easily into the worst pitfall of the spiritual life: self-hatred and self-judgment; instead of focusing on the good God, the God of mystery and love in whose gaze I see only God's love for me and for everything created by that loving glance.[6]

I can hear—can't you?—in that searching self-assessment an echo of what St. Francis himself said so often at the end of his life of extreme asceticism, "Let us begin, brothers, to serve the Lord our God, for up to now we have hardly progressed."

Not long ago, I witnessed the marriage of a couple who met after college while serving in AmeriCorps. He had been my parishioner and so invited me to Knoxville, Tennessee, for the ceremony, which was ecumenical in nature. Before embarking on their own careers, both bride and groom generously had separately decided to spend a year or two of their lives serving others. They brought to their marriage these beautiful values. No doubt organizations such as AmeriCorps and the Jesuit Volunteers, among many others, are fulfilling a new generation's desire for service. They are also, like the early Franciscan movement, providing community living for people who want to share their gifts with others. These communities may be temporary, but they are significant in terms of the new evangelization.

Stewardship and the New Evangelization

For many years now the Church, especially in the United States, has been striving to introduce to parishes the biblical practice of stewardship. According to the Bible, tithing means setting aside the first 10 percent of our annual income and offering it to God. God, in other words, does not merely receive the leftovers after we have done what we want to do with our resources. Sometimes stewardship takes the form of giving 5 percent of income annually to the Church and the other 5 percent to charities of our choice. Regardless of how, specifically, this 10 percent is divided, stewardship is a tangible expression of the priority of God in our lives.

While stewardship of our resources is only a part of our embrace of the Gospel way of life and evangelical poverty, it must find its proper place in the new evangelization. The bottom line is that we must become more thoughtful about how we live and expend not only our treasure but also our time and our talent in service of God and others, especially those most in need.

I find it encouraging that here in the United States major philanthropists such as Warren Buffet and Bill and Melinda Gates have publicly committed themselves to—after having taken proper care of their families—giving away their entire fortunes. The new evangelization should be an opportunity to unleash this kind of generosity, to find common ground among nonbelievers, common ground which can lead us all closer to the person of Christ, whom Cardinal Dulles found at the center of the Christian attraction. Pope Francis's challenge to the whole Church remains truer than ever: "How I would like a church which is poor and for the poor!"

EIGHT

LOVE OF THE EARTH, OUR HOME, AND ALL ITS CREATURES

In his lovely book *Poets in a Landscape*, the classicist Gilbert Highet places poems and poets in the landscape from which they emerged as a necessary avenue into the Latin poetry he celebrates. Among those poets is Propertius, born about 50 BC. His home was Umbria, the region of Italy that is identified with St. Francis and he with it. Francis is forever known, not just as Francis, but as Francis of Assisi. Here is how Highet describes their landscape:

> North of Rome, the land changes. It becomes richer and more fertile, but also bolder and stranger. The rocky Apennine backbone of Italy sends out curving ribs and throws up harsh vertebrae of stone. There are high ridges of hill, with cool glens and forests among them. There are fruitful planes, often commanded by steep spurs of rock which have always made splendid natural fortresses. It is not an easy country to travel through, even now. It was hard for conquerors in the past to unite it, or to dominate and assimilate it. The Romans themselves scarcely succeeded in doing so after centuries of tough fighting. Later, in the Middle

Ages, it was broken up among dozens of small feuding communities, each with its own fortress-center, its own walls, castle, flag and history. It is not united to this day. But it is full of rich individuality, of glorious traditions, and of noble art.[1]

Assisi lies close to the Rieti Valley, where St. Francis spent most of his time—a valley then of forests with chestnut and oak trees and lots of birds. To the best of our knowledge it was in 1225, near the end of his life while he was awaiting an eye operation for his failing eyesight, that Francis wrote his famous "Canticle of the Creatures." We might note that most of Italy, including Umbria, is now mostly deforested, and there are almost no birds except pigeons, since Italians capture and eat birds.

St. Francis's "Canticle of the Creatures" is truly remarkable. It is the earliest example of lyric poetry composed in the Italian language. It was written when the saint was in great discomfort from his many illnesses and near death. In fact, he added the final lines about "Sister Death" shortly before he died. But most of all, the canticle is justly admired because God is praised not just *as* the Creator of all things but *through* the created things themselves. Landscape painters have coined the phrase "nature *morte*," "dead nature," but for Francis all of nature, even the rocks, were alive, and each in its own way beautiful, mirroring the beauty of God.

Brother Leo, a companion of Francis, once said, "God tamed his wild creatures for Francis because Francis loved them so much." According to Bonaventure, Francis wished to return "to the state of original innocence through universal reconciliation with each and every thing."[2] Some of the examples Bonaventure provides, however, strain our imaginations.

Take the case of the worshipping sheep. It seems that at the Portiuncula, his precious "little portion" of a dwelling in Assisi, he was once given a sheep, which he admired for its innocence and simplicity and thus gratefully accepted. Francis taught the sheep to praise God and not disturb the friars. The sheep followed these instructions so well that when the friars were chanting before the altar the sheep would genuflect and bleat along with them. When at Mass the sacred host was elevated, the sheep went down on two bended knees!

Then there is the story of Francis preaching to the birds, telling them to stop their racket until the friars had finished chanting the canonical hours. According to Bonaventure, "At once they were silent and remained in silence as long as it took the friars to say the hours at length and to finish their praises."[3]

There is also the falcon that became his solicitous companion and caregiver during his forty-day fast at La Verna. The falcon took on the task of waking Francis during the night for his usual time of prayer, but when the bird observed that Francis needed more sleep because of his declining health, "the falcon had pity and did not impose such early vigils on him."[4]

But, of course, the most famous of these tales involves the ravaging wolf of Gubbio, a tale with wide ecological implications. This story is found among the *fioretti*, the "little flowers" collected about St. Francis's life.

> At the time when St. Francis was living in the city of Gubbio, a large wolf appeared in the neighborhood, so terrible and so fierce, that he not only devoured other

animals, but made a prey of men also; and since he often approached the town, all the people were in great alarm, and used to go about armed, as if going to battle.

St. Francis, however, felt great compassion toward the oppressed people of the town and offered to go and meet the wolf for a conversation. Everyone advised against such a move as too dangerous. St. Francis nonetheless set out with some friars and also the people watching at a safe distance.

The wolf charged toward the saint with open jaws. Making the sign of the cross over the wolf, St. Francis said, "Come here, brother wolf. I command you in the name of Christ neither to harm me nor anyone else." Marvelous to tell, no sooner had St. Francis made the sign of the cross, that the terrible wolf, closing its jaws, stopped running, and coming up to St. Francis, lay down at his feet as meekly as a lamb.

St. Francis then preached repentance to the wolf and made him promise that if the people agreed to feed him from then on, the wolf would no longer attack any animal or human being. The wolf lifted up its right paw and placed it in St. Francis's hand, "giving him thereby the only pledge which was in his power." The people looked on with astonishment at this miracle.

The story concludes: "The wolf lived two years in Gubbio; he went familiarly from door to door without harming anyone, and all the people received him courteously, feeding him with great pleasure, and no dog barked at him as he went about."[5]

A park in Santa Fe, New Mexico, has a life-size bronze statue of St. Francis addressing an attentive prairie dog—a nice adaptation!

The lesson here seems clear. Nature rebels when it is not cared for. We can only think, for example, of global warming, which most good science shows that we engender through the accumulated emissions we humans carelessly send into the atmosphere. We increasingly witness the result: newly destructive storms and devastating heat waves drying up crops and producing potential famine.

Oftentimes the Christian take on our ecological responsibilities is based upon the notion of stewardship, referenced in the book of Genesis: speaking to the first humans, God says, "Have dominion over the fish of the sea, the birds of the air, and all the living things that move on the earth." God then continues: "See, I give you every seed-bearing plant all over the earth and every tree that has seed-bearing fruit on it to be your food; and to all the animals of the land, all the birds of the air, and all the living creatures that crawl on the ground, I give all the green plants for food." (Gn 1:28–29). Therefore God made the first humans in his own "image, after our own likeness" (Gn 1:26), a remarkable assertion, especially in the Old Testament, where all images of God are forbidden. God is understood to make human beings his stand-ins in the care of creation. Therefore God can "rest" after all his creating was done, for God has entrusted to us the stewardship of all God has made. But, as we know, God has been having nightmares ever since.

Instead of this familiar image of stewardship to describe our relationship with nature, St. Francis speaks of *kinship*: all the creatures are our brothers and sisters. In the numerical symbolism of his time, based upon the seven liberal arts, the first set of three creatures—the sun, the moon, and the stars—represent grammar, rhetoric, and dialectic and simultaneously have the Christian symbolism of faith, hope, and charity. The second set of four creatures—wind, air, water, and fire—stand for arithmetic, geometry, music, and astronomy as well as the four cardinal virtues of prudence, justice, temperance, and fortitude. Thus the whole of creation manifests a stupendous order and beauty mirroring God.[6]

Creation becomes more than something to merely *master*, since it enunciates the masterly artistry of God.

> *The Canticle of the Creatures*
> Most High, all powerful, all good Lord!
> All praise is yours, all glory, all honor
> And all blessing.
>
> To you alone, Most High, do they belong.
> No moral lips are worthy
> To pronounce your name.
>
> All praise be yours, my Lord, through all you
>   have made,
> And first, my lord Brother Sun,
> Who brings the day, and light you give us
>   through him.
>
> How beautiful is he, how radiant in all
>   his splendor!
> Of you, Most High, he bears the likeness.
>
> All praise be yours, my Lord, through Sisters
>   Moon and Stars;
> In the heavens you have made them,
> Bright and precious and fair.
>
> All praise be yours, my Lord, through Brothers Wind and Air,

All fair and stormy, all the weather's moods,
By which you cherish all that you have made.

All praise be yours, my Lord, through
    Sister Water,
So useful, lowly, precious and pure.

All praise be yours, my Lord, through
    Brother Fire,
Through whom you brighten up the night.
How beautiful is he, how gay! Full of power
    and strength.

All praise be yours, my Lord, through Sister
    Earth, our mother,
Who feeds us in her sovereignty and produces
Various fruit with colored flowers and herbs.

All praise be yours, my Lord, through those
    who grant pardon
For Love of you; through those who endure
Sickness and trial.

Happy those who endure in peace;
By you, Most High, they will be crowned.

All praise be yours, my Lord, through
    Sister Death,
From whose embrace no mortal can escape.

Woe to those who die in mortal sin!
Happy those She finds doing your will!
The second death can do no harm to them.

Praise and bless the Lord, and give
    him thanks,
And serve him with great humility.

Contemporary Applications

The Cherokee nation has but one word to express land, religion, history, and culture. These all have to do with rootedness in a place, a particular place in the universe where we find our deepest identity. The science of the care for Earth, our home, appropriately is called "ecology," which literally means "the science of the house." In Psalm 84 we read, "How lovely your dwelling, O Lord of Hosts. Blessed are those who dwell in your house." Our beautiful blue and green planet is our house, our home, and it is also the home of God. St. Augustine said that God wrote two books, creation and scripture, and God would not have written the second if we were aware of his presence in the first.

In a recent lecture sponsored by the National Endowment for the Humanities, the eminent ecologist Wendell E. Berry based his remarks on the place he and his family have called home for generations: Henry County, Kentucky. He used the metaphors of "boomers" and "stickers" to contrast contemporary relations with the environment we share. Boomers are those who pillage and run, and stickers are those who settle and love the life they have made and the place they have made it on. The boomer, he said, is motivated by greed, the desire for money and property, and therefore power. Stickers, on the contrary, are motivated by affection, by such love for a place and its life that they want to preserve it and remain in it.

Berry then goes on to speak about the irreplaceable function of imagination, which he defines as the full consciousness of the verb "to see." He continues:

> I will say, for my own belief and experience, that imagination thrives on contact, on tangible connection.

For humans to have a responsible relationship to the world, they must imagine their places in it. To have a place, to live and belong in a place, to live from a place without destroying it, we must imagine it. By imagination we see it illuminated by its own unique character and by our love for it. By imagination we recognize with sympathy the fellow members, human and non-human, with whom we share our place. By that local experience we see the need to grant a sort of preemptive sympathy to all the fellow members, the neighbors, with whom we share the world. An imagination enables sympathy, sympathy enables affection. And it is in affection that we find the possibility of a neighborly, kind and conserving economy.[7]

What better description could we have of St. Francis of Assisi and his warm, sympathetic relationship with nature?

"You have to see it to save it," Thomas Friedman concluded in his book, *Hot, Flat, and Crowded*. "If I've learned anything about ecology," Friedman says, "it is that all conservation is local."[8] "Locavores" is a new word referring to those who seek their food close to home as opposed, say, to eating kiwis anytime of the year, since this would require that the food be shipped from New Zealand, a phenomenon which results in an exorbitant use of fuel. These people's focus is on local gardens, local farmers' markets, and local loyalties.

The Catholic Climate Covenant for the care of the creation and the care of the poor is a new environmental initiative. The Catholic Climate Covenant, which identifies our carbon footprint as part of our moral living on this planet, seeks to show respect for God's creation by highlighting the link between creation and poverty, embodied in the life and ministry of St. Francis of Assisi. Its aim is to get as many as possible to sign on to the St. Francis Pledge to Care for Creation and the Poor. The five elements of the pledge are as follows:

1. Prayer for creation and the poor
2. Learning more about climate change as a moral issue
3. Assessing one's participation in contributing to the climate crisis
4. Acting to change behaviors and attitudes
5. Advocating Catholic social principles and practices[9]

Back in 2001 I was part of a drafting committee for the United States Conference of Catholic Bishops that produced the groundbreaking statement "Global Climate Change: A Plea for Dialogue, Prudence, and the Common Good." Since then the issue of climate change has become even more acute, but many Christians relegate the climate crisis to the end of their list of priorities. More than ever, therefore, we need St. Francis's intercession.

At a Bible discussion I was conducting, some members of the group who were Evangelical Christians from Texas shared their anxiety about the droughts that were afflicting their region of the country. "What is God trying to tell us in all this?" they asked me. Trying to express what may be on the mind of God in any particular situation is never easy. In my first attempt at an answer, I gave examples of how natural disasters can result in unforeseen blessings. When my own local community experienced a power outage that deprived our homes of heat and light for five days because of a severe storm, the usually reticent and private New Englanders reached out to each other beyond their normal comfort zone. I told them how people meeting each other in the post office might say, "If you need to shower, come to our house. We still have power." However, a more complete answer to their question about what God might be trying to call to their attention through these increasingly frequent droughts is that this is *not* normal; this is climate change, and we are responsible for it. Perhaps that part of the response might have been more difficult to hear and to accept.

Among the Final Propositions from the Synod of Bishops on the New Evangelization is a greater attention in evangelization to what the synod calls "the path of beauty." The bishops cite St. Augustine's claim that "it is not possible to love what is not beautiful." They go on to say, "Beauty attracts us to love, through which God reveals to us his face."[10] The bishops mention art, and surely God's greatest artistic expression is creation itself. John Muir, whose preservation efforts led to the establishment of Yosemite National Park, once wrote, "Everybody needs beauty as well as bread, places to play in and pray in, where nature may heal and give strength to body and soul alike."

The inaugural Mass of Pope Francis coincided with the Feast of St. Joseph, patron and protector of the universal Church. Pope Francis chose as the theme of his homily for this occasion the vocation of the Christian to be a protector in all its dimensions. He exhorted, "Let us protect Christ in our lives, so that we can protect others, so that we can protect creation!" He continued:

> The vocation of being a "protector," however, is not just something involving us Christians alone; it also has a prior dimension which is simply human, involving everyone. It means protecting all creation, the beauty of the created world, as the Book of Genesis

tells us and as Saint Francis of Assisi showed us. It means respecting each of God's creatures and respecting the environment in which we live. It means protecting people. . . . In the end, everything has been entrusted to our protection, and all of us are responsible for it. Be protectors of God's gifts![11]

On the occasion of World Environment Day, which was sponsored by the United Nations in June 2013, Pope Francis devoted his entire address at his weekly public audience to the religious and moral dimensions of the environment. He began appropriately by citing his predecessor Pope Benedict XVI, who was often called the "green pope." He noted that Benedict frequently called attention to our responsibility to respect "the rhythm and logic of God's creations which is God's free gift, a love story between God and ourselves. This love story should evoke in us the attitude of wonder, contemplation, and listening."

Pope Francis then sharply criticized what he called the greatest danger to creation we face—the unethical, single-minded pursuit of money. "Man is not in charge today, money is," he stated. "God our Father did not give the task of caring for the earth to money but to us, men and women. We have this task! Instead men and women are sacrificed to the idols of profit and consumption, the culture of waste." He continued:

> The "culture of waste" tends to become the common mentality that infects everyone. Human life, the person, is no longer perceived as a primary value to be respected and protected, especially the poor and disabled, if not yet useful—such as the unborn child—or no longer needed—such as the elderly.

This culture of waste has made us also insensitive to the waste and disposal of food, which is even more despicable when all over the world, unfortunately, many individuals and families are suffering from hunger and malnutrition. We should all remember that the food we throw away is as if stolen from the table of the poor, the hungry![12]

Francis here is echoing the homily of St. Basil in which he declared that the bread we clutch in our hands belongs to the starving, the cloak we keep locked up in the closet belongs to the naked, and the shoes we are not using belong to the barefoot.

NINE

LOVE OF PEACE AMONG ALL PEOPLES AND RELIGIONS

In the summer of 1219 St. Francis undertook a third dangerous journey to the Middle East. His two previous attempts had failed because of storms and other catastrophes. His aim was ambitious: to hold a conversation with Sultan Malik al-Kamil, who lived just outside the city of Damietta in Egypt and who was known in the West as a cruel tyrant. The circumstances were not favorable, to say the least. For more than one hundred years, popes and civil rulers had mounted one Crusade after another in order to liberate the Holy Land from Muslim control. The crusaders succeeded in this attempt in 1099, but eighty years later the Muslims took it all back. During the Fourth Crusade those involved pillaged Constantinople and stole many of the treasures of the Christian Byzantine Empire. The Fifth Crusade was launched by Pope Innocent III in September 1217. His plan was to attack Egypt and deprive the Muslims of their wealth and navy. In one month, October 1218, three thousand of Sultan Malik al-Kamil's troops were slaughtered in battle with the crusaders.

Under the leadership of Cardinal Pelagius Galvani, the pope's delegate, the siege of Damietta and its eighty thousand people was still continuing when St. Francis and his companions arrived in Egypt. Cardinal Pelagius was firing up the troops, calling the Muslims "a perfidious and worthless people."[1] In his account of the visit of Francis with the sultan, St. Bonaventure attributes two causes to Francis's drive to hold this conversation: a personal desire to become a martyr and the hope to convert the sultan to Christianity. He reports a challenge that the saint made to the sultan, a literal trial by fire reminiscent of Elijah and the prophets of the Hebrew Bible. Once a bonfire was lit, Francis and some priests of Islam would walk through the flames. God would protect the defender of the true faith. The sultan demurred, upon which Francis, according to Bonaventure, said that he would walk through the flames alone to convince the sultan he should become a Christian. Once again the sultan refused, claiming he would lose his position among his own people should he become a Christian.[2] The *fioretti* tell the same version of the story and make the claim that the sultan ultimately accepted to be baptized.[3]

We get another interpretation of the visit entirely from the second biography of the saint by Thomas of Celano. According to Celano, Francis's intent was peace between the religions of Christianity and Islam and an end to what he perceived to be a potentially disastrous attack on Damietta. This interpretation seems to be the consensus of modern Franciscan scholarship.

Francis's attempt to intervene during the Fifth Crusade should be viewed in the context of his constant opposition to warfare and the pride and avarice that often cause it. He preferred not to argue. His message to the powers of the day was delivered largely, but not solely, by his counter-cultural example of a life of poverty, compassion, and non-violence. His dedication to peace confronted the violent culture of his day. "At a time when the wealthy engaged in falconry, he preached to the birds."[4]

In light of Francis's commitment to the priority of wit-ness over words, we should see even more clearly how great was Francis's desire for peace that he should travel so far to speak with the sultan. Celano explains that the Christians of Egypt, the Coptic Orthodox and the Melkites, were suffering greatly because of the Christian attacks on their homeland. The Muslim authorities destroyed many of their churches and imposed extra taxes upon them. Pri-or to his meeting with the sultan in August 1219, Francis became aware of a new assault planned by the crusaders. Jesus appeared to him and told him to oppose the attack. Following his conscience, Francis opposed the plan. *Deus vult*, "God wills it," was the rationale of the Crusades. Francis dared to say, "God does not will this." The soldiers decided to ignore this warning from a disreputable and unknown friar. Nonetheless, Francis held to his judgment: "Let the princes of this world know that it is not easy to fight against God."[5]

In the meantime the sultan offered new peace propos-als. Francis and Brother Illuminato decided to go in person to meet the sultan—no weapons, no letter of protection, across a landscape of rotting corpses and destruction. The two friars, not knowing the native tongue, kept shouting "Sultan! Sultan!" Amazingly, they were brought into the sultan's presence.

Al-Kamil was then thirty-nine years of age, Francis half a year younger. They formed an immediate bond. Francis gave his usual greeting: *"Pace e bene,"* "Peace and good welfare." The sultan inquired whether Francis was there as an ambassador of the pope. "We are ambassadors of the Lord Jesus Christ," Francis responded. The sultan then allowed Francis, this simple, unlettered man dressed in rags, to preach in the presence of his advisers.

For eleven days Francis and the sultan engaged in religious dialogue. Francis and Brother Illuminato were treated as honored guests all the while. The sultan even gave Francis the key to his private prayer room. Before their departure, the sultan hosted a lavish banquet in their honor and offered them precious gifts in admiration of the evident holiness of his guests. Francis declined them all except for a horn of ivory that he took with him to Assisi and used thereafter to summon the people to prayer. Francis had shown the sultan the mark of a true Christian: not an avaricious monster or murderer, but, on the contrary, one who can love an enemy.

As an additional pledge of admiration, the sultan gave Francis and his friars the right to access the holy places in Jerusalem without paying any tribute. He gave them safe passage back to their camp. It is believed that Francis took the sultan up on his offer and visited Jerusalem before his journey back to Italy.

Upon his return, Francis wrote the following instruction to the friars regarding their relations with Muslims:

> The brothers who go can conduct themselves among them spiritually in two ways. One way is to avoid quarrels and disputes and to be subject to every human creature for the sake of God, so bearing witness

to the fact that they are Christians. Another way is to proclaim the word of the gospels when they see it as God's will, calling on their hearers to believe in God almighty, Father, Son and Holy Spirit, that they may be baptized and become Christians.[6]

Francis's journey to Egypt and his experience of Islam introduced further changes. Upon returning, he instituted the practice among the friars of kissing the floor of every church they entered, a practice he had seen Muslims do in their mosques.

After the culminating experience of his life, the impression of the stigmata of Christ upon his body, Francis asked Brother Leo to give him pen and paper so he could compose a prayer. The prayer was very much like the Muslim prayer celebrating the ninety-nine beautiful names of God, names that are counted out on a string of prayer beads. In the Qur'an we read that God is the compassionate, the merciful, the sovereign, the most holy, the peaceful, the mighty, the creator, the forgiver, the provider, the generous. Francis had evidently learned much from his stay in the East.

At the bottom of this parchment, Francis drew a figure lying upon the ground looking up to heaven. He placed the letter *tau* in his mouth. Upon close inspection, the prone, bearded figure wearing a turban seems to be Sultan Malik al-Kamil. Behind him Francis had drawn a crude map of Egypt and its coastline leading to Jerusalem. The drawing seems to illustrate a prayer that God would protect Francis's friend the sultan. This parchment is still kept on the lower level of the Basilica of St. Francis in Assisi.

A recent biography of the saint makes this observation about his remarkable encounter with the sultan:

In Assisi is preserved an ivory horn thought to be the gift of the sultan to Francis. The pledge of brotherhood between these two men is surely the most remarkable the world has ever seen. One can well believe that if this horn should sound again, the spirit of St. Francis would return to us, so thoughtful and loving that no one could resist his call, ancient and ever new.[7]

What has become known as the "Prayer of St. Francis" is most probably a much later composition, but its every word and phrase radiate the spirit of the one to whom history has attributed it:

> Lord, make me an instrument of your peace.
> Where there is hatred let me sow peace.
> Where there is injury let me sow pardon.
> Where there is doubt let me sow faith.
> Where there is despair let me give hope.
> Where there is darkness let me give light.
> Where there is sadness let me give joy.
>
> O Divine Master, grant that I may not try to
>   be comforted
> but to comfort, not try to be loved but to love.
> Because it is in giving that we receive,
> it is in forgiving that we are forgiven,
> and it is in dying that we are born to eternal
>   life.

CONTEMPORARY APPLICATIONS

Islam is the fastest-growing religion in the world. It has been for some time. No doubt much of its phenomenal growth has to do with its utter simplicity. On its most basic level it consists of five actions. The first is the profession of faith, the *shahada*: "I bear witness that there is no god but God and I bear witness that Muhammad is God's messenger." The second obligation is to pray facing Mecca five times a day: at dawn, noon, midafternoon, sunset, and early night. These prayers must be said in Arabic, which Muslims believe to be the language God used to dictate the Qur'an. Certain body postures accompany the prayers—standing up, bowing, prostration, and sitting, all according to a particular order. These prayer positions replicate the vision Muhammad had upon his ascension into heaven: he saw ascending choirs of angels each praising God in one of these ways. Again according to Muslim tradition, Muhammad also conversed upon his rise with Adam, Abraham, and Jesus.

The third obligation-action is to tithe at least 2.5 percent of your wealth to religious and charitable causes. The fourth is to fast from dawn to sunset during the month of Ramadan, refraining from eating, drinking, and sexual relations. The fifth is to make the *hajj* or pilgrimage to Mecca.

In his book *Moving the Mountain: Beyond Ground Zero to a New Vision of Islam in America*, the imam Feisal Abdul Rauf expresses the hope that Americans will gain a better understanding of Islam and reject its many caricatures as extremist, judgmental, retrograde. He writes,

> I almost wish we could use the ancient language and call ourselves "believers" rather than Muslims. In our zeal to exalt our own religions, we lost sight of what we have in common, which is deeper than any particular manifestation of a religious faith. . . . If all of us, including today's Muslims, were to return to thinking of ourselves as believers in this larger sense, it would

expand the space for more interfaith interaction and mutual respect among those who consider themselves believers.[8]

On October 26, 1986, Blessed John Paul II invited leaders from all the religions of the world to assemble together in Assisi and pray for peace. The formula chosen was that the leaders of the various religious traditions would come together to pray—not pray together. This was to avoid a weak syncretism, a watered-down version of each person's faith and prayer. It was an amazing witness to present to the world in the very city of St. Francis. Catholicism itself, with this precedent-shattering initiative, took on a new profile in the world of being a unifying force for peace among all religions and peoples.

The Catholic Church also has the example of Blessed Charles de Foucauld, the former French legionnaire who served in North Africa. Born into a wealthy family, Foucauld, like St. Francis, lived a military life until his adult conversion to his childhood faith. I recall one day being in Paris and visiting the Church of Saint-Augustin and discovering a plaque in one of the confessionals that read, "It was here that Charles de Foucauld was converted to Christ." Ordained a priest in the Trappist order, he chose to live a hermit's life in Algeria among the Muslims whose faith he admired so much.

Foucauld embodied the spirituality of presence. According to this spirituality, simply *being* a Christian—without preaching—should be enough to convince others of the beauty of the Christian faith and the love a Christian must practice toward all people. Foucauld was killed by terrorists in 1916 and was declared blessed by Pope John Paul II in 2005. Although Foucauld in the eyes of Muslims must always be associated with the French colonial enterprise among so-called barbarians, he represents the irreplaceable value of personal contact across ethnic and religious lines as the only path toward real dialogue and religious understanding.

Jesus' encounter with the Samaritan woman beautifully illustrates this new way of evangelization by means of conversation, dialogue, and affirmation. The Gospel of John tells us that to go from Judea to Galilee Jesus "had to pass through Samaria" (Jn 4:4). Actually, he could have skirted hostile Samaria, as many Jews did, but Jesus chose otherwise. In a town called Sychar he sat down, tired, next to Jacob's well at around noon. A Samaritan woman happened to be coming to the well to draw water, a common domestic task for women. Jesus initiated the conversation.

"Give me a drink," he said. The Samaritan woman was taken back: "How can you, a Jew, ask me, a Samaritan woman, for a drink?" It was not only that Jesus was a Jew, but he was also a rabbi, and a rabbi could never speak with a woman in public, much less a Samaritan woman who was regarded as a half-breed and a heretic.

Jesus replied: "If you knew the gift of God and who is saying to you, 'Give me a drink,' you would have asked him and he would have given you living water" (Jn 4:10).

This is an example of a "two-level" conversation that is characteristic of the Gospel of John: Jesus is speaking on a profoundly spiritual level, and his partner is mired in a material way of thinking. They do not talk to one another at this point but past each other. Another example is the conversation between Jesus and Nicodemus. Jesus tells him, "No one can see the kingdom of God without being born from above." Nicodemus, missing the whole spiritual meaning of Jesus' words, replies with utter literalness, "How can a person once grown old be born again? Surely he cannot reenter his mother's womb and be born again, can he?" (Jn 3:3–4).

And so the woman replied to Jesus, "Sir, you do not even have a bucket and the cistern is deep; where then can you get this living water? Are you greater than our father Jacob, who gave us this cistern and drank from it himself with his children and his flocks?" (Jn 4:11–12). A light was beginning to dawn in the mind of the Samaritan woman: this is no ordinary man.

Jesus patiently continued: "Everyone who drinks this water will be thirsty again; but whoever drinks the water I shall give will never thirst; the water I shall give will become in him a spring of water welling up to eternal life" (Jn 4:13–14).

The woman remained on the material level, however, and made the banal request, "Sir, give me this water, so that I may not be thirsty or have to keep coming here to draw water" (Jn 4:15).

Jesus gave up. He tried another tack. "Go call your husband and come back," he told her. The woman answered him truthfully: "I do not have a husband." Jesus then revealed his knowledge of her life and its sad condition. "You are right in saying, 'I do not have a husband.' For you have had five husbands, and the one you have now is not your husband. What you have said is true" (Jn 4:17–18).

The woman was stricken in her heart. She was beginning to understand something of her mysterious conversation-partner's nature. "Sir, I can see that you are a prophet," she said in awe (Jn 4:19). She then dared to raise the religious question that is at the heart of the divide between

Jews and Samaritans such as herself. She was now deeply engaged and opened her heart. "Our ancestors worshiped on this mountain; but you people say that the place to worship is in Jerusalem" (Jn 4:20). Mount Garizim loomed over them as they spoke, the place of Samaritan worship. Samaritans accepted the Pentateuch of Moses but rejected the Jewish prophets and the Temple worship in Jerusalem.

Jesus replied:

> "Believe me, woman, the hour is coming when you will worship the Father neither on this mountain nor in Jerusalem. You people worship what you do not understand; we worship what we understand, because salvation is from the Jews. But the hour is coming, and is now here, when true worshipers will worship the Father in Spirit and truth; and indeed the Father seeks such people to worship him. God is Spirit, and those who worship him must worship in Spirit and truth." (4:21–24)

The woman then confided, "I know that the Messiah is coming, the one called the Anointed; when he comes, he will tell us everything" (Jn 4:25).

Then Jesus revealed to her, a Samaritan woman, something he had not yet revealed to anyone else: "I am he, the one who is speaking to you" (Jn 4:25).

The woman was overwhelmed. She did something uncharacteristic then: she left behind one of her most precious possessions, her family water jar, and hurried back to the town. She told the townspeople, "Come see a man who told me everything I have done. Could he possibly be the Messiah?" (Jn 4:29). This brought people out of the town, and they made their way toward him.

The woman of Samaria had become an evangelist. Jesus had gently affirmed her religious seeking and absolved her of her failings, something only the long-anticipated Messiah could do. She wanted everyone to meet him.

In June 1962, during a pilgrimage to the Holy Land with other newly ordained priests, I visited Samaria. Jacob's well, where Jesus and the Samaritan woman conversed, still exists. Mount Garizim still looms nearby. While there, we were immediately surrounded by a group of Samaritans asking us for help. They knew we were Christians and so they told us we had to be kind to them just as Jesus was. Didn't he make the hero of one of his parables "the good Samaritan?"

A similar method of evangelization was practiced by St. Patrick, who in bringing Christianity to a "pagan" environment endorsed certain elements of the spirituality he found, elements which connected God and nature without being pantheistic. For Patrick, the religion of Jesus was no "enemy" to this profound spirituality but its affirmation and fulfillment.

In his annual address to the Roman curia in December 2011, Pope Benedict XVI referred to two rules generally accepted today as fundamental for interreligious dialogue:

1. Dialogue does not aim at conversion but at understanding.
2. Both parties to the dialogue remain consciously within their identity, which the dialogue does not place in question.

Benedict went on to make the point that dialogue also must engage the issue of the truth. He continued: "To be sure, we do not possess the truth, the truth possesses us.

Christ, who is the truth, has taken us by the hand, and we know that his hand is holding us securely on the path of our quest for knowledge. . . . At one with him, we stand in the light of truth."[9]

TEN

MODERN *FIORETTI*

When I was living in Italy in 1982, a group of Italian journalists and writers put together a collection of what they called *Fioretti vivi di San Francesco nell'arte naive*: "Living Fioretti of St. Francis in Art Done in the Naive Style."[1] When I was presented with this hefty volume, I was also given one of the artworks illustrated within it. It depicts a young man lying prostrate on the floor of a church in Malta. He is pronouncing vows of poverty, chastity, and obedience in the presence of his parents, who watch from the side. From this beautiful book I got the idea of collecting a few contemporary stories of my own that would depict one or another aspect of Franciscan spirituality alive today.

FIORETTO 1

The October 19, 2012, edition of the *New York Times* ran a story about eight postcollege youth living a communal life in an intentional Christian community in Tucson, Arizona.[2] Each member of the community commits to two years teaching in a Catholic school whose population is among the poorest in the city. They are given a monthly stipend of a thousand dollars by the Alliance for Catholic Education.

The Alliance for Catholic Education was established by the University of Notre Dame in 1993. Notre Dame provides graduate courses in pedagogy, Catholic theology and social teaching to prepare young teachers from various colleges for their mission.

A chaplain to the program described it this way, "It's like what the disciples of Jesus did, sent out to teach and live in their countries." One of the teachers profiled in the story said, "I didn't go to a Catholic college and until now I was only an occasional church participant, but I did want to give something back. This work, praying together at home, has made me grow."

FIORETTO 2

In October 2008 I was in San Francisco for the dedication of the first national shrine in honor of St. Francis of Assisi in the city named for him. On the occasion, an exact replica of the Portiuncula, St. Francis's "little portion" in Assisi, was dedicated.

The small chapel was constructed entirely in Assisi and reassembled in San Francisco. Several of the laborers who constructed it came to the dedication, as did the mayor of Assisi, who was the principal speaker for the occasion.

The mayor knew no English, so his words had to be translated as he spoke. His message was simply this: God does not dwell in big things but in small ones. That truth is what St. Francis taught and lived.

Fioretto 3

One day I was walking to the subway in New York City and entered the station at Christopher Street. On the lower level, just outside the entrance, I noticed out of the corner of my eye a man lying on the floor begging. I passed him and went to the turnstile to swipe my card. I swiped several times and nothing happened.

Apparently the beggar had been watching and noticed my frustration. He called over to me, "Here, use my card," and handed it to me.

I told this story to two Franciscans who belong to a small, new community called the Franciscans of Primitive Observance. We met in a train station in Boston, and the three of us sat together on the train going north. Over their gray habits each was wearing a warm-up jacket that was well-worn. Although it was winter, they had no socks under their sandals. I inquired why they were not hitchhiking. They said, "Oh, you know about us." They explained that they had accepted a train ticket to give a youth retreat but since, like Francis, they must beg for food and travel without money they usually walked or hitchhiked to their destinations. They matched my story with one of their own (one of many, they said) from their hitchhiking adventures.

A man picked them up, and when he left them off he pressed into one of their hands what they discovered to be a hundred-dollar bill. Since, according to their rule, they could not keep the money, they decided to spend some of it for a meal at McDonald's. While there, they needed to use a cell phone and asked several of the other patrons if they could use theirs. Having been rebuffed by the seventh person they asked, they noticed a homeless man pulling out a cell phone from his pocket. They asked him if they could use his phone, and he agreed. Thanking him, they pressed into his hand seventy dollars, what they had left of the gift given to them.

FIORETTO 4

One of my parishioners used to attend Saturday evening Mass with her daughter, a reluctant participant. As a treat afterward, the mother would take her daughter out for a meal. During the meal the mother would ask what the daughter had gotten out of the scripture readings and the homily. Usually it wasn't much.

But one evening over dinner the mother got a surprise. They had noticed a man outside who was begging. "Here," the mother said to her daughter, "take this money outside and give it to that man for a meal."

Back at the table, the mother said, "You see, this is what Mass is all about." The daughter replied, "No, Mother, this is not what Mass is all about. If we had invited him to have dinner with us, that is what the Mass is all about."

FIORETTO 5

I was seated in Market Square in Knoxville, Tennessee, with members of a wedding party. I was witnessing the wedding the next afternoon. It was July and extremely hot—the temperature at midday around 98 degrees. As we sat at our table in the open air, a motley group of beggars, some disguised as entertainers, passed by. One was an Elvis Presley imitator. Another seemed to be selling newspapers. Another was a violinist. But the one that caught my eye was an elderly black man with a white scraggly beard who wore little more than rags for clothing.

By a rope, the elderly beggar was leading, at a solemn pace, a dog of no particular breed. On the dog's head was perched a green parrot. Sadly, not one of the diners around Market Square seemed to notice. Then the beggar gently took the green parrot from the dog's head and placed it in his mouth. The bird then emerged again totally calm.

I wished Flannery O'Connor might have been there to observe the scene with me. Surely she could have derived and depicted the mysterious workings of divine grace we were witnessing. O'Connor once said, "You will have found Christ when you are concerned with other people's sufferings and not your own."

FIORETTO 6

As was my custom at the late afternoon Christmas Eve Mass attended by children, their parents and other relatives, during the reading of the gospel Christmas story I assembled a pageant of children portraying the various roles. We would even have a live baby, if one happened to have born around Christmas. I cheated a little and included the three Wise Men to provide opportunity for greater participation.

But for me, and perhaps for the congregation, the highlight of the pageant was the participation of live animals, in imitation of St. Francis, who used live animals in the first *persepio* ever. Sometimes the sheep meekly came down the center aisle at the proper time—oftentimes not! There even was the occasional accident on the carpet. One

Christmas a sheep got loose and had to be wrestled to the ground by its keeper.

In such circumstances Jesus Christ was born.

FIORETTO 7

New Mexico, I discovered, is a place where people often go for a second life. Georgia O'Keeffe was one such person. Her clear, sharp rendering of the desert and its exotic flowers is a testimony to the clarity of vision she achieved in these spectacular surroundings. Another was the much-married aristocrat from the East, Mabel Dodge Luhan, who once said, "Now I have come to the place where one life ends and another begins." We stayed at her house in Taos, which is now a bed and breakfast.

New Mexico is rich in Franciscan heritage. The cathedral in Santa Fe is named for St. Francis. There are still remnants here and there of the unsanctioned shrines of the flagellants (penitential associations of lay people) who, though diminished in numbers, still continue today to beat themselves in repentance for their sins. Religious art of the region contains reminders of the Matachine dancers who performed similar penitential acts. The crucifixes are graphic in their depictions of the crucified Lord's sufferings. All of this, however, seems at odds with the sophisticated art scene and the wholesomeness of the farmers' markets that proliferate.

And yet, the sparkling gambling casinos that are everywhere in New Mexico and the alcohol abuse that is prominent here—to mention only two modern vices—call for a repentance that will truly make possible that second life, a place where one life ends and another begins.

FIORETTO 8

One of my parishioners, a grandmother, proudly showed me a poem written by her eight-year-old granddaughter. She was so proud of the poem that she gave it to a professor at the Harvard Divinity School, who in turn read it to his class. It could have come, it seemed to me, from St. Francis's "Canticle of the Creatures."

> *Dandelion*
> *By Tyler S.*
> Dandelion grows in
> A field. Everyday, it grows more.
> Now, it is sunshine yellow!
> Dandelion starts to get old.
> Every day, it gets whiter,
> Lying in the grass,
> Imagining how pretty it was when it was
>   yellow.
> Oh, wind! Blowing the seeds away.
> Now, all of the white seeds are flying!

FIORETTO 9

The front gate of our local Franciscan monastery boasts this sign:

> Franciscan Monastery and Guest House.
>   No pets allowed.

What more need I say?

Fioretto 10

Among the many stories that circulated after the election of Pope Francis was one told by the kiosk owner in Buenos Aires where Cardinal Jorge, as he was known, got his daily newspaper. Once Pope Francis was elected, the kiosk owner was stunned with disbelief when he received a phone call from someone who identified himself as Cardinal Jorge telling him to cancel his newspaper delivery. Another of the many things that struck him about Cardinal Jorge had to do with the rubber bands that he put around the newspapers to keep them from being blown away when they were delivered to the cardinal. At the end of each month, the cardinal always returned the rubber bands, all thirty of them.

The kiosk owner said he gets goose bumps whenever he thinks about the simplicity of Pope Francis.

Fioretto 11

At the 2013 Chrism Mass, Cardinal Sean O'Malley, O.F.M. Cap., of Boston recounted how the gospel story of the poor widow's mite played itself out one day in Bolivia:

> Once as a young priest I was unvesting in the sacristy after Mass when a young Bolivian lad came in and handed me a hundred dollar bill. This is the first time this happened in that parish. I said, "What is this?" and he explained he had found it in the parking lot. I was surprised that anyone who would have been in that lot would have had a hundred-dollar bill. I knew the boy and his family. I had just recently baptized his little sister Shirley who had Down Syndrome. Their

father had recently abandoned the mother and five children who were undocumented immigrants and were living in deplorable conditions. I went and spoke with the mom, Anita, who was waiting with the other children. I said, "Anita, do you have any money?" She said, "No, Father," and then, "Actually I had five dollars I was going to use to buy food, but then I heard today's gospel about the widow's mite. So, I decided to put it in the collection." I gave Anita the hundred-dollar bill and said, "I think God wants you to have this. If anyone shows up looking for their hundred dollars, I'll take care of it." Needless to say, no one ever came.

TWO BETHLEHEMS

Sixteen of us were ordained in Rome fifty years ago. We returned to the city in December 2011 to celebrate the anniversary. With Christmas soon approaching, we traveled two-and-a-half hours by bus from Rome to Umbria and the tiny hill town of Greccio. It was precisely here, on Christmas night, 1223, that St. Francis of Assisi assembled the first *persepio*, with Mass offered in a cave on an altar erected over hay and between an ox and an ass. The steep, tiny paths of the village were challenging enough for our aging group (one of us using a walker), but we had not counted on this being the shrine's busiest day in the entire year. Flocks of children, many in scout uniforms, filled the spaces, all of which almost made us forget that Italy has zero population growth.

On that night in 1223, Francis had just returned from his renowned pilgrimage to the Holy Land. As our thirty-five-year-old Franciscan guide explained, the saint wanted to recreate—as much as he could back at home—the full sensuous experience of contemplating the birth of the Son of God as a baby. "I want to remember," he is recalled as saying, "that the child was born in Bethlehem and see with my own earthly eyes the hardship of his humble infancy, how he slept in the manger and how he was laid on the hay between the ox and the ass." The friar said Francis kept repeating over and over in his native Italian, "*Il bambino Gesu' e' nato a Betlemme*," savoring each syllable for its sweet sound: "The baby Jesus has been born in Bethlehem."

One of Francis's biographers wrote, "On Christmas night, men and women from all of the surrounding areas climbed the mountain with candles and torches that filled the night sky with light. Greccio became a new Bethlehem." From our bus I noticed a sign at the foot of the hill leading to the village that declares, "*A Greccio, ogni giorno e' Natale*": "In Greccio, every day is Christmas day." That was the point of the *persepio* in the first place in the mind of Francis: Christmas is not the recollection of a past event in human history, something that took place in some remote part of the world; Christmas can happen now, here, to me.

In the fourteenth century the wall of the cave where St. Francis recreated the birth of Christ was decorated by a painting that portrays a tender, intimate moment. Mary removes her breast from her red dress to feed her child, who amazingly stands up on his own feet to receive nourishment. Our Franciscan guide explained that displaying a naked breast like that was not conventional at the time and that the red color of Mary's dress symbolized the Holy Spirit by whose power Mary conceived her divine child.

As it happened, in the month before our visit to Greccio and Rome, on November 4 I spent the day with a group of pilgrims in the actual Palestinian town of Bethlehem. To cross the barbed-wire barrier into Bethlehem, we had to pass the inspection of Israeli soldiers armed with machine guns, mostly youth fulfilling compulsory military service. We were told by our Arab guide, who was an Israeli citizen, that almost 50 percent of the occupied Palestinian territory has been made into Israeli settlements. We saw one of these massive new housing projects under construction near our checkpoint. Once inside the barrier, we found numerous beggars on the streets; unemployment is high.

Christian pilgrims are blessed in that most of the holy sites associated with the life of Jesus, including the place of his birth, are in the custody of Franciscans as well as of various Orthodox Churches. Since the control of the Holy Land by the Ottoman Empire, many of the major places of pilgrimage, including the ancient buildings constructed over the actual place of Jesus' birth, have been entrusted to the Orthodox. The Holy Land today is no Disneyworld, but it is a spiritual place where all humanity seems to come together. We stood in line for more than three hours just to stoop down and enter the tiny space where it is said Jesus was born, and to kiss the silver star in the floor, before being rushed off by the Orthodox priest in charge. I thanked him in English for performing this trying duty.

The discordance between the two Bethlehems, the one in Greccio and the one in Palestine, is enormous: the place of religious imagination and the experience of divine sweetness and tender love, and the place of history surrounded with barbed-wire barricades. Just before Christmas recently, newspapers reported a scuffle between two of the Orthodox communities caring for the shrine of the Nativity. Each jealously guarding its own territory to be cleaned in the shrine before the Christmas celebrations began, the robed priests hurled brooms and pans at one another until they were separated by Palestinian police. Soon after Christmas, still another point of tension between Israelis and Palestinians emerged with the announcement of plans by Israelis to construct a new tourist center and parking garage in East Jerusalem. This is where the Palestinian Authority wants its future capital to be.

By coincidence, the homily of Pope Benedict XVI on Christmas night 2011 focused upon Greccio and its *persepio*. The pope noted how St. Francis

> kissed images of the Christ-child with great devotion and stammered tender words such as children say. For God's Son to take the form of a child, a truly human child, made a profound impression on the heart of the Saint of Assisi, transforming faith into love. . . . Francis loved the child Jesus because for him it was in this childish estate that God's humility shone forth. God became poor.[1]

Reflecting upon the appearance of God in the form of a helpless child, Pope Benedict said, "God pits himself against all violence and brings a message that is peace." Then he prayed:

> At this hour, when the world is continually threatened by violence in so many places and in so many different ways, when over and over again there are oppressors' rods and bloodstained cloaks, we cry out to the Lord: O mighty God, you have appeared as a child. . . . We love your childish estate, your powerlessness, but we suffer from the continuing presence of violence in the world, and so we ask you: manifest your power, O God, in this time of ours, in this world of ours . . . that your peace may triumph in this our world.[2]

Happily, there are in this world of ours some real places such as Greccio where every day is Christmas day, where one can experience what peace is like. This is what gives us hope that someday the Bethlehem of dreams and the Bethlehem of history will at last become one.

In his first encyclical, Pope Francis highlights committed Christians who have bravely faced the suffering in the world and, by their example, helped people bear it. He writes:

> Nor does the light of faith make us forget the sufferings of this world. How many men and women of faith have found mediators of light in those who suffer! So it was with Saint Francis of Assisi and the leper, or with Blessed Mother Teresa of Calcutta and her poor. They understood the mystery at work in them. In drawing near to the suffering, they were not able to eliminate all their pain or explain every evil. . . . Faith is not a light that scatters all our darkness, but a lamp which guides our steps in the night and suffices for the journey.[3]

My friends whom I visited in Santa Fe live in a city with a distinctive Franciscan flavor. The *persepio* first imagined by St. Francis is now part of everybody's Christmas. My prayer and hope, my reason for writing this book, is to help them and many others to explore his life and see its real connection with their own. The Christmas crib was not just a personal devotion of St. Francis but also a brilliant method of evangelization.

Joan Acocella, writer for *The New Yorker* magazine, recently reviewed two new biographies of St. Francis. She began her review by recalling his very unusual and appealing human personality:

Francis was scrawny and plain-looking. He wore a filthy tunic, with a piece of rope as a belt, and no shoes. While preaching, he often would dance, weep, make animal sounds, strip to his underwear, or play the zither. His black eyes sparkled. Many people regarded him as mad, or dangerous. They threw dirt at him. Women locked themselves in their houses.

Francis accepted all this serenely, and the qualities that at the beginning had marked him as an eccentric eventually made him seem holy. His words, one writer said, were "soothing, burning, and penetrating." He had a way of "making his whole body a tongue." Now, when he arrived in a town, church bells rang. People stole the water in which he had washed his feet; it was said to cure sick cows.

Years before he died, Francis was considered a saint, and in eight centuries he has lost none of his prestige. Apart from the Virgin Mary, he is the best known and most honored of Catholic saints.[4]

Jesus himself was considered by his contemporaries as both appealing and "crazy." We read in the Gospel According to Mark, "He came home. Again [the] crowd gathered, making it impossible for them even to eat. When his relatives heard of this they set out to seize him, for they said, 'He is out of his mind'" (Mk 3:20–21). To become so in love with the God of Creation, so united with the Cross of his Son, and so attuned to his Spirit that we come to be perceived as "out of our minds," is, it seems, the true test of life.

NOTES

INTRODUCTION

1. Pope John Paul II, Apostolic Letter *Novo Milenio Inuente*, January 6, 2001, http://www.vatican.va/holy_father/john_paul_ii/apost_letters/documents/hf_jp-ii_apl_20010106_novo-millennio-ineunte_en.html.

2. Synod of Bishops, *Instrumentum Laboris*, 2012, Preface, http://www.vatican.va/roman_curia/synod/documents/rc_synod_doc_20120619_instrumentum_xiii_en.html.

3. Synod of Bishops, *Synodus Episcoporum Bulletin*, October 28, 2012, 23, http://www.vatican.va/news_services/press/sinodo/documents/bollettino_25_xiii-ordinaria-2012/02_in-glese/b33_02.html.

4. Pope Paul VI, Apostolic Exhortation *Evangelii Nuntiandi*, (London: Catholic Truth Society, 1975), 41.

5. Bonaventure, *The Soul's Journey into God, The Tree of Life, The Life of St. Francis*, trans. Ewart Cousins (New York: Paulist, 1978), xv.

1. A SAINT FOR TODAY

1. G. K. Chesterton, *St. Francis of Assisi* (Garden City, NY: Image, 1957).

2. Ibid., 9–18.

3. Joseph Bottum, "New World Pope," *Weekly Standard*, March 25, 2013, 13.

4. Adrian House, *Francis of Assisi: A Revolutionary Life* (Mahwah, NJ: Hidden Spring, 2001), 7.

5. John O'Malley, S.J., *The History of the Popes from Peter to the Present* (New York: Rowan & Littlefield, 2011), 127.

6. Lynn White, quoted in House, *Francis of Assisi: A Revolutionary Life*, 10.

7. Marina Warner, quoted in House, *Francis of Assisi: A Revolutionary Life*, 9.

8. Pope Francis, "Audience to Representatives of the Communications Media," March 16, 2013, http://www.vatican.va/holy_father/francesco/speeches/2013/march/documents/papa-francesco_20130316_rappresentanti-media_en.html.

9. Pope Francis, "Homily in the Sistine Chapel," March 14, 2013, http://www.vatican.va/holy_father/francesco/homilies/2013/documents/papa-francesco_20130314_omelia-cardinali_en.html.

10. Bonaventure, *Life of St. Francis*, 179.

11. Sophocles, *The Cure at Troy: A Version of Sophocles' Philoctetes*, trans. Seamus Heaney (New York: Farrar, Straus, and Giroux, 1961).

2. "My House Is Falling Down"

1. Gay Talese, "The Crisis Manager," *New Yorker*, September 24, 2012, 44–45.

2. Pope Francis, *Lumen Fidei*, June 29, 2013, 8, http://www.vatican.va/holy_father/francesco/encyclicals/documents/papa-francesco_20130629_enciclica-lumen-fidei_en.html.

3. Arnaldo Fortini, *Francis of Assisi*, trans. Helen Moak (New York: Crossroad, 1981), 42.

4. Anthony Mockler, *Francis of Assisi: The Wandering Years* (New York: E. P. Dutton, 1997), 77.

5. Thomas of Celano, *The Francis Trilogy* (New York: New City Press, 2004) I, xv, 38.

6. Ibid., viii, 18.

7. Fortini, *Francis of Assisi*, 229.

8. Bonaventure, *Life of St. Francis*, 208.

9. "Prophet for our times," *Tablet*, September 8, 2012, 2, http://www.thetablet.co.uk/article/163172.

10. Pope Francis, "Homily on the Solemnity of Saint Joseph," March 19, 2013, http://www.vatican.va/holy_father/francesco/homilies/2013/documents/papa-francesco_20130319_omelia-inizio-pontificato_en.html.

3. "The Dragon Is in Charge of the City"

1. Madeline Levine, *Teach Your Children Well: Parenting for Authentic Success* (New York: Harper, 2012).

2. *Catechism of the Catholic Church*, Second Edition (Vatican City: Libreria Editrice Vaticana, 1997), 1869.

3. Pope Francis, "Address to the New Non-Resident Ambassadors to the Holy See," May 12, 2013, http://www.vatican.va/holy_father/francesco/speeches/2013/may/documents/papa-francesco_20130516_nuovi-ambasciatori_en.html.

4. Pope Francis, *Lumen Fidei*, 50–51.

4. "Preach the Gospel Always. If Necessary, Use Words"

1. Celano, *The Francis Trilogy*, II, 207.

2. Bonaventure, *Life of St. Francis*, 236.

3. House, *Francis of Assisi: A Revolutionary Life*, 236.

4. Pope Francis, "Homily on Holy Thursday," March 28, 2013, http://www.vatican.va/holy_father/francesco/homilies/2013/docments/papa-francesco_20.

5. Ibid.

6. Pope Francis, "Address during Way of the Cross," March 29, 2013, http://www.vatican.va/holy_father/francesco/speeches/2013/march/documents/papa-francesco_20130329_via-crucis-colosseo_en.html.

7. Bonaventure, *Life of St. Francis*, 194–95.

8. Dom Roger Hudleston, trans., *The Little Flowers of St. Francis of Assisi* (Westminster, MD: Newman, 1953), 22.

9. Pope Francis, "Homily on Palm Sunday," March 24, 2013, http://www.vatican.va/holy_father/francesco/homilies/2013/documents/papa-francesco_20.

10. Sergio Luzzatto, quoted in "The Strange Victory of Padre Pio" by Alexander Stille, review of *Padre Pio: Miracles and Politics in a Secular Age*, by Sergio Luzzatto, *New York Review of Books* 59, no. 16, (October 25, 2012): 32.

11. Pope John Paul II, quoted in the review of *Padre Pio*.

12. Sergio Luzzatto, quoted in the review of *Padre Pio*.

5. The Gospel Way of Life

1. Bonaventure, *Life of St. Francis*, 5.

2. Ibid., 292–93.

3. Wallace Stevens, *Collected Poetry and Prose* (New York: Library of America, 1997), 8.

4. Pope Francis, "Homily," April 7, 2013, http://www.vatican.va/holy_father/francesco/homilies/2013/documents/papa-francesco_20130407_omelia-possesso-cattedra-laterano_en.html.

6. Love of God and God's Poor

1. Bonaventure, *Life of St. Francis*, 304–5.

2. Ibid., 223.

3. Francis of Assisi, "Testament," in *Francis of Assisi—The Saint: Early Documents* I, eds. Regis Armstrong, J. A. Wayne Hellmann, and William Short (New York: New City Press, 1999), 124.

4. Bonaventure, *Life of St. Francis*, 190.

5. Francis of Assisi, "A Letter to the Entire Order," 28–29, *Francis of Assisi—The Saint: Early Documents I*, 118.

6. Bonaventure, *Life of St. Francis*, 315.

7. Pope Benedict XVI, *Deus Caritas Est* (Vatican City: Libreria Editrice Vaticana, 2006), 14, 25.

8. Pope Benedict XVI, *Caritas in Veritate* (Vatican City: Libreria Editrice Vaticana, 2009), 1.

9. Ibid., 2.

10. Ibid., 39.

11. Ibid., 6.

12. Ibid., 34.

13. Ibid., 37.

14. Ibid., 53.

15. The Hour Exchange, http://www.hourexchangeportland.org.

16. *Isabel de Bertodano,* "The Bergoglio I knew," *Tablet,* April 16, 2013, 4, http://www.thetablet.co.uk/article/164020.

17. Avery Dulles, S.J., *A Testimonial to Grace and Reflections on a Theological Journey: Fiftieth Anniversary Edition* (Kansas City: Sheed and Ward, 1996), 38.

18. Ibid., 89.

19. *Dei Verbum*, 5.

20. Dulles, *A Testimonial to Grace*, 89.

7. Love of Poverty in Imitation of Jesus

1. Bonaventure, *Life of St. Francis*, 199–200.

2. Ibid.

3. Ibid., 315.

4. Peter Brown, *Through the Eye of a Needle: Wealth, the Fall of Rome, and the Making of Christianity in the West, 350–550 AD* (Princeton, NJ: Princeton University Press, 2012), xxv.

5. Pope John Paul II, "Homily in New York," October 2, 1979, http://www.vatican.va/holy_father/john_paul_ii/homilies/1979/documents/hf_jp=ii_hom_19791002_usa-newyork_en.html.

6. Murray Bodo, O.F.M., *The Threefold Way of Saint Francis* (New York: Paulist, 2000), 23, 25.

8. Love of the Earth, Our Home, and All Its Creatures

1. Gilbert Highet, *Poets in a Landscape* (Harmondsworth, UK: Penguin Books, 1959), 82.

2. Bonaventure, *Life of St. Francis*, 250.

3. Ibid.

4. Ibid., 256–60.

5. Hudleston, *Little Flowers of St. Francis of Assisi*, 50–53.

6. Paul M. Allen and Joan deRis Allen, *Francis of Assisi's Canticle of the Creatures: A Modern Spiritual Path* (New York: Continuum, 1996).

7. Wendell E. Berry, "Lecture," National Endowment for the Humanities, April 24, 2012, http://www.neh.gov.

8. Thomas L. Friedman, *Hot, Flat, and Crowded* (New York: Farrar, Straus, and Giroux, 2008), 303, 315.

9. See catholicclimatecovenant.org.

10. Synod of Bishops, *Synodus Episcoporum Bulletin*, October 28, 2012, 20, http://www.vatican.va/news_services/press/sinodo/documents/bollettino_25_xiii-ordinaria-2012/02_inglese/b33_02.html.

11. Pope Francis, "Homily, Solemnity of Saint Joseph," March 19, 2013, http://www.vatican.va/holy_father/francesco/homilies/2013/documents/papa-francesco_20.

12. Pope Francis, "Audience," June 5, 2013, http://en.radiovaticana.va/news/2013/06/05/pope_at_audience:_counter_a_culture_of_waste_with_solidarity/en1-698604.

9. Love of Peace Among All Peoples and Religions

1. Paul Moses, *The Saint and the Sultan: The Crusades, Islam and Francis of Assisi's Mission of Peace* (New York: Doubleday, 2009), 89.

2. Bonaventure, *Life of St. Francis*, 268–70.

3. Hudleston, *Little Flowers of St. Francis of Assisi*, 55–57.

4. Moses, *Saint and the Sultan*, 3.

5. Ibid., 119.

6. Ibid., 163.

7. Fortini, *Francis of Assisi*, 4, 35.

8. Feisal Abdul Rauf, *Moving the Mountain: Beyond Ground Zero to a New Vision of Islam in America* (New York: Free Press, 2012), 35–36.

9. Pope Benedict XVI, "Christmas Message to the Curia," December 21, 2012, http://www.vatican.va/holy_father/benedict_xvi/speeches/2012/december/documents/hf_ben-xvi_spe_20121221_auguri-curia_en.html.

10. Modern *Fioretti*

1. Calisto Fornero, ed., *Fioretti vivi di San Francesco nell'arte naïve*, (Italy: Nuova Abes, 1982).

2. Samuel G. Freedman, "Serving Needy Schools, Brothers and Sisters of the 21st Century," *New York Times*, October 20, 2012, http://www.nytimes.com/2012/10/20/us/young-catholic-teachers-united-in-service.html?_r=0.

Conclusion: Two Bethlehems

1. Pope Benedict XVI, "Homily," December 24, 2001, http://www.vatican.va/holy_father/benedict_xvi/homilies/2011/documents/hf_ben-xvi_hom_20111224_christmas_en.html.

2. Ibid.

3. Pope Francis, *Lumen Fidei*, 57.

4. Joan Acocella, "Rich Man, Poor Man. The Radical Vision of St. Francis," *New Yorker*, January 14, 2013, 72.

Monsignor Charles M. Murphy is the director of the permanent diaconate for the Diocese of Portland, Maine. He is the author of a number of scholarly articles and several books, including *Eucharistic Adoration, The Spirituality of Fasting, At Home on the Earth, Wallace Stevens: A Spiritual Poet in a Secular Age,* and *Belonging to God.* Murphy is the former academic dean and rector of the Pontifical North American College in Rome and served as part of the editorial group working in Italy under Cardinal Ratzinger on the third draft of the *Catechism of the Catholic Church,* which became the fourth and final version.

Murphy serves as consultant to the United States Conference of Catholic Bishops committee on catechetics, reviewing materials for conformity with the Catechism. He served as chair of the editorial committee that produced the pastoral letter on environmental issues by the Bishops of the Boston Province and as a consultant to the USCCB for their statement on global warming. He has been the pastor of four parishes in Maine and has served his diocese in ecumenical and educational capacities. Murphy holds a doctorate in sacred theology from the Gregorian University, a master's degree in education from Harvard University, and a bachelor's degree in classics from the College of the Holy Cross.

Founded in 1865, Ave Maria Press,
a ministry of the Congregation of
Holy Cross, is a Catholic publishing
company that serves the spiritual and
formative needs of the Church and its
schools, institutions, and ministers;
Christian individuals and families; and
others seeking spiritual nourishment.

For a complete listing of titles from

Ave Maria Press

Sorin Books

Forest of Peace

Christian Classics

visit www.avemariapress.com

ave maria press® / Notre Dame, IN 46556
A Ministry of the United States Province of Holy Cross